A Supplement to *A Dictionary of Irish Saints*

A SUPPLEMENT TO

A Dictionary of
Irish Saints

Containing Additions and Corrections

Pádraig Ó Riain

FOUR COURTS PRESS

Typeset in 10.5pt on 12pt DantePro by
Carrigboy Typesetting Services for
FOUR COURTS PRESS LTD
7 Malpas Street, Dublin 8, Ireland
www.fourcourtspress.ie
and in North America for
FOUR COURTS PRESS
c/o IPG, 814 N. Franklin St, Chicago, IL 60610

A catalogue record for this title is available
from the British Library.

ISBN 978-1-80151-019-6

Printed in Ireland by
SprintPrint, Dublin.

CONTENTS

PREFACE

In the eleven years since its publication by Four Courts Press in 2011 *A dictionary of Irish saints* has rarely been far, either from my mind or from my desk. Beginning with notes added to an interleaved copy, followed by entries in red in the online copy generously provided by Four Courts Press, I have since assembled a large selection of supplementary material, which, to my mind, merits being brought to the attention of those who own a copy of the first edition. It is hoped that a future second edition of the *Dictionary* will include this material. In the meantime, however, the Press has kindly agreed to make available in this format the material assembled to date.

In addition to those named in the original work, the following have provided valuable further information: Cormac Bourke, George Cunningham, Jeremy Cunningham, Fidelma Maguire, Joseph Mannion, Pádraig Ó Cearbhaill, Conchubhar Ó Crualaoich, Julian Walton and Laurence Walsh OCSO. My colleagues at the Locus Project, Kevin Murray and Emma Nic Cárthaigh, have continued to assist in identifying the locations of churches associated with saints. Kevin Murray also read and commented very helpfully on the present work. The supplement has also profited from helpful comments made by reviewers of the *Dictionary* and, as I plan to continue correcting and adding to entries, I would be very grateful for further recommendations from users of the present list or, indeed, of the original *Dictionary*. As heretofore, Dagmar Ó Riain-Raedel has continued to encourage my work on the *Dictionary* throughout. Finally, I wish to thank Sam Tranum of Four Courts Press, who carefully copy-edited the text and made several valuable suggestions.

In what follows, additions and corrections are shown in red.

ADDITIONAL SOURCES

AbEMLS   *Above and beyond: essays in memory of Leo Swan*, ed. T. Condit & C. Corlett (Dublin, 2005).

ACE   *Archdiocese of Cashel and Emly: Pobal Ailbhe*, C. O'Dwyer (Strasburg, 2008).

AHWD   *Ancient and holy wells of Dublin*, G. Branigan (Dublin, 2012).

AMW   Archives of the Marquis of Waterford, Curraghmore House.

AmraeCC   *Amrae Coluimb Chille: a critical edition*, J. Bisagni (Early Irish Text Series 1; Dublin, 2019).

BAil.   *Beatha Ailbhe: the Life of Saint Ailbhe of Cashel and Emly*, ed. P. Ó Riain, ITS 67 (London & Dublin, 2017).

CHSC   *Celtic hagiography and saints' cults*, ed. J. Cartwright (Cardiff, 2003).

CKV   *Clerics, kings and vikings: essays on medieval Ireland in honour of Donnchadh Ó Corráin*, ed. E. Purcell, P. MacCotter, J. Nyhan & J. Sheehan (Dublin, 2015).

CL   *A carnival of learning*, ed. P. Harbison & V. Hall (Roscrea, 2012).

Colk.Cat.   *Trinity College library Dublin: Descriptive catalogue of the medieval and Renaissance manuscripts*, M.L. Colker, 2 vols (London, 1991).

CSI   *Church and settlement in Ireland*, ed. J. Lyttleton & M. Stout (Dublin, 2018).

DDé   *Dán Dé: the prose poems of Donnchadh Mor O Dálaigh, and the religious poems in the duanaire of the Yellow Book of Lecan*, ed. L. McKenna (Dublin, n.d.).

DDSC   *Davnet and Dympna: a single cult*, S. Ó Dufaigh (Castleblaney, 2021).

DKil   *The diocese of Kilmore 1800–1950*, D. Gallogly (Cavan, 1999).

EIRD   *Ex ipsis rerum documentis: Beiträge zur Mediävistik*, ed. K. Herbers, H.H. Kortüm & C. Servatius (Sigmaringen, 1991).

EMH   *The early medieval hand-bells of Ireland and Britain*, C. Bourke (Dublin, 2020).

FC   *Famulus Christi: essays in commemoration of the thirteenth centenary of the birth of the Venerable Bede*, ed. G. Bonner (London, 1976).

FIO   *Fursa's Irish origins: Munster, Connacht or Ulster?*, P. Ó Riain (Fursey Occasional Paper 6; Norwich, 2015).

GILSL   *Gaelic Ireland (c.600–c.1700): lordship, saints and learning*, ed. L. McInerney & K. Simms (Dublin, 2021).

HMDC   *A history of the medieval diocese of Cloyne*, P. MacCotter (Dublin, 2013).

IIAM   *L'irlanda e gli irlandesi nell' alto medioevo*, Settimane di Studio lvii (Spoleto, 2010).

IP   *I, Patricius: the Roman history of an Irish saint*, P. Colling Egan (Maysville, MO, 2020).

ADDITIONAL SOURCES

JIA	*Journal of Irish archaeology*, 1 (1983–).
Keimelia	*Keimelia: studies in medieval archaeology and history in memory of Tom Delaney*, ed. G. Mac Niocaill & P.F. Wallace (Galway, 1988).
LegSS	*Legends of Scottish saints: readings, hymns and prayers for the commemorations of Scottish saints in the Aberdeen Breviary*, ed. A. Macquarrie (Dublin, 2012).
LF 3	*Lost and found III: rediscovering more of Ireland's past*, ed. J. Fenwick (Dublin, 2018).
LME	*Logainmneacha Mhaigh Eo*, 10 vols, F. Mac Gabhann (Baile Átha Cliath, 2014).
LnaL	*Lorg na leabhar a festschrift for Pádraig A. Breatnach*, ed. C. Breathnach, M. Ní Úrdail & G. Ó Riain (Dublin, 2019).
MartFC	*Add*: ed. P. Ó Riain.
MartR	*The martyrology of the Regensburg Schottenkloster*, ed. P. Ó Riain (HBS 124, London, 2019).
MedAE	*Medium Aevum* (1932–).
MHA	*Medieval hagiography: an anthology*, ed. T. Head (London, 1999).
MSNAF	*Mémoires de la Société nationale des Antiquaires de France* 1 (1872).
MWPSS	*Medieval Welsh poems to saints and shrines*, ed. B. Lewis (Medieval and Modern Welsh Series xiv; Dublin, 2015).
NL	*Northern lights: following folklore in north-western Europe*, ed. S. Ó Catháin et al. (Dublin, 2001).
NSW	*The North Sea world in the Middle Ages: Studies in the cultural history of north-western Europe*, ed. T.R. Liszka & L.E.M. Walker (Dublin, 2001).
PCNT	*The parish churches of north Tipperary: commemorating a two-hundred-year heritage*, W.J. Hayes & J. Kennedy (Roscrea, 2007).
PnaB	*Párliament na mban*, ed. B. Ó Cuív (Dublin, 1952).
PPPMI	*Princes, prelates and poets in medieval Ireland: essays in honour of Katharine Simms*, ed. S. Duffy (Dublin, 2013).
Propug.CV	*Propugnaculum catholicae veritatis, libris X. constructum*, A. Bruodinus, 2 vols (Digitized copy of Prague, 1669 edition).
RIGI	*Royal inauguration in medieval Ireland c.1100–1600*, E. Fitzpatrick (Woodbridge, 2004).
RIW	*Relics and the Insular world, c.600–c.800*, Julia M.H. Smith, Kathleen Hughes Memorial Lectures 15 (Cambridge, 2017).
RT	*The rule of Tallaght*, ed. E. Gwynn, *Hermathena* 44 (1927).
SacH	*Sacred histories: a festschrift for Máire Herbert*, ed. J. Carey, K. Murray & C. Ó Dochartaigh (Dublin, 2015).
SBDeer	*Studies on the Book of Deer*, ed. K. Forsythe (Dublin, 2008).
SBK	*Saint Brigid of Kildare: life, legend and cult*, N. Kissane (Dublin, 2017).
SCorn.	*The saints of Cornwall*, N. Orme (Oxford, 2000).
TBF	*Transitus beati Fursei*, O. Rackham (Norwich, 2007).
TC	*Tiarnach of Clones*, S. Ó Dufaigh (Mullaghmurphy, Co. Monaghan, 2018).

TEAB   *The end and beyond medieval Irish eschatology*, 2 vols, ed. J. Carey, E. Nic Cárthaigh & C. Ó Dochartaigh (Aberystwyth, 2014).

TEP   *Two epistles of St. Patrick the bishop*, P. Colling Egan (Maysville, MO, 2021).

TMD   *Tales of medieval Dublin*, ed. S. Booker & C.N. Peters (Dublin, 2014).

TNW   *Logainmneacha na hÉireann iv: townland names of co. Wexford: ainmneacha na mbailte fearainn co. Loch Garman*, ed. C. Ó Crualaoich & A. Mac Giolla Chomhghaill, 2 vols (Dublin, 2016).

TOAS   *Transactions of the Ossory Archaeological Society* 1–3 (1874–83).

UL Camb. University Library Cambridge.

VCol.   *Ionae vitae sanctorum Columbani, Vedastis, Iohannis*, Scriptores Rerum Germanicarum in usum scholarum ex Monumentis Germaniae Historicis separatim editi (Hannover & Leipzig, 1905).

VFBA   *The Vita Fursei and its Use by Bede and Aelfric*, A. Casey (Fursey Occasional Paper 5; Norwich, 2010).

WBP   *The writings of Bishop Patrick 1074–1084*, A. Gwynn (Dublin, 1955).

INTRODUCTION

Add: The cults of Fursa and Faolán flourished in Ireland, most notably in the Galway churches of Killursa and ~~Kiltullagh~~ 'Killilan' in Cahertinny townland, parish of Kilconickny, where they appear to have [p. 46, ll 4–5]

DICTIONARY ENTRIES

ABÁN

Add: The saint's cult appears to have spread also to Doonane in the parish of Rathaspick, adjoining Killabban, Leixlip in Kildare [p. 52, ll 27–8]

Add: Finally, it has recently been shown that a quatrain in Irish cited in the saint's Life, which is preserved separately in a manuscript copied in Waterford in the thirteenth century, was regarded as a charm to ensure safe passage for marine travellers.[18] [p. 52, end of entry]

Add (to) notes: **10** *PPPMI* 333–7; *LnaL* 100. **18** *LnaL* 95–112.

ADHAMHNÁN

Add: the Breviary of Aberdeen, and a set of *mionannála*, 'minor annals', relates how, as a youth, the saint foretold the accession of his *anamchara*, 'soul-friend', Fionnachta *Fleadhach* 'of the feasts' († 695), to the kingship of Tara, before later foretelling the dire consequences of the king's failure to observe his summons to a meeting.[18] [p. 54, l. 35]

Add: 'an angel of the Lord'.[20] In addition to some *canones*, mainly dealing with alimentary regulations, several poems [p. 54, l. 41]

Add: church of Donaghmoyne, and his bell, known as the *Dubh Díoghlach*, may have been kept at Skreen in Co. Sligo.[25] [p. 55, l. 6]

Add: Born, according to the annals in 624, the saint died in 704 [p. 55, l. 9]

Add: Adhamhnán's relics were brought to Ireland in 727, when his Law was renewed, and brought back to Iona in 730.[31] A relic of the saint, accompanied by relics of Colum Cille and Finnian of Movilla, had reached Saint-Maurice d'Agaune in the Swiss canton of Valais by the second half of the eighth century.[32] [p. 55, end of entry]

Add (to) notes: **1** *BiblSS* i, 199–201; *VC*[1], xl–lxviii. **18** *LegSS* 232–3, 318–20; *SG* i, 403–6. **21** *Kenney* 245. **25** *EMH* 483 §219. **31** *AU s.a.* **32** *RIW* 13, 32.

AIGHLEANN

Add: Another sister, Machain, alias 'Machua', is described as patron of Shanagarry in the parish of Kilmahon (probably from Irish Ceall Mhachain) in a late eighteenth-century list of Cloyne parishes.[5] [p. 58, end of entry]

Add (to) notes: **4** *PRC* 28, 50. **5** *CPR* i, lxviii; *HMDC* 10.

AILBHE of Emly

Add: Ailbhe is said to have died in either 527, 534 or 542. [p. 60, l. 5]

Add: both Stowe Missal litanies, and his role as defender of Munster is exemplified in a prophetic poem, which describes how he expels hordes of Saxons.[26] [p. 60, l. 12]

Add to notes: **1** *BiblSS* i, 635–7. **5** *BAil.* 72 §22. **7** *BAil.* 60–72 §§4–21. **10** *BAil.* 70–2 §21. **11** *BAil.* 72–4 §§23–7. **12** *BAil.* 74–8 §§29–34. **13** *BAil.* 78–86 §§36–50. **14** *BAil.* 86 §49. **20** *BAil.* 58 §2. **16** *VSHP* ii, 69–70 §§21–2. **25** *EMH* 484 §220. **26** *EAB* 719 §§15–16.

AILBHE of Shancough
Add: 'St Eliva', who is venerated at Toberelva in the Roscommon parish of Baslick, probably also represents this cult.[10] [p. 61, end of entry]
Add note: **10** *OSL RN* i, 165.

AILFINUS
Add: An early seventeenth-century description of the diocese of Derry names the patron of the Donegal church as 'Aghenagus'.[3] [p. 61, end of entry]
Add note: **3** *AnH* 12, 107, 109.

AODH OF FOYRAN
Add to note: **3** *ILL* 247.

AODH OF RAHUGH
Add: Aodh died, according to the annals in 589 and, although 10 November [p. 68, l. 18]
Add to notes: **1** *BiblSS* i, 628–9. **9** cf. *CSI* 17–31. **24** *AU s.a.*

AODH of Sleaty
Add: Aodh's genealogy, which names his father as Brocán, attaches him to the Uí Bhairrche of north Carlow.[7] [p. 69, end of entry]
Add (to) notes: **1** *BiblSS* i, 629–31. **7** *CGSH* §245; *BiblSS* i, 631.

AODHAMAIR
Add/read: an ecclesiastical site at Killaughan (Ceall Aodhamair Shoghain) in the parish of ~~Killaughan~~ Ballymacward, barony of Tiaquin.[3] [p. 71, l. 13 of entry]

AODHÁN of Eachradh
Add: Alternatively, the reference may be to the Laois townland of Agharra in the parish of Erke.[4] [p. 72, l. 8 of entry]
Add note: **4** Logainm.ie 'Agharra'. [Renumber note 4 to 5]

AODHÁN of Kilmore
Add: Apart from his alleged occupancy of the see of Clogher, little else is known of the saint. [p. 74, l. 11 of entry]
Add to note: **4** *Cl.Rec.* 7, 380.

AODHÁN of Lindisfarne
Add: the saint's tomb and holy well. [p. 75, l. 7]
Add: and a short office Life is contained in the Breviary of Aberdeen.[10] [p. 75, l. 10]
Add to notes: **1** *BiblSS* i, 625–7. **9** *PNCL* 230, 236. **10** *LegSS* 208–11, 321–2.

AODHÁN of Templeshanbo
Read: things.[3] Aodhán died, according to the annals, in 563 (or 570) and John Colgan suggested, speculatively, that ~~Aodhan's~~ his feast fell either on 1 January or 9 October.[4] [p. 75, ll 10–11 of entry]
Add to note: **4** *AU s.a.*

AOIDHGHIN of Bodoney

Add to note: 1 *BiblSS* i, 646–7.

AONA

Add/read: While in Inis Ainghin, now ~~Hare Island~~ Hareisland on Lough Ree, or in Inis Clothrann, now Inchcleraun on the same lake, Ciarán [p. 77, ll 9–10 of entry]

Add: Killeedy, who is said to have died in the same year (570 or 570) as Aona, describes [p. 77, ll 13–14 of entry]

Add to notes: 2 *AB* 69, 98–9. 5 *AU s.a.* 6 *VSHH* 232–3, 392. 7 *SG* i, 401.

Add after **Aonghas** of Clonmacnoise: **Aonghas** of Connor. *See* Mac Nise of Connor.

AONGHAS LÁIMHIODHAN

Add: The *sanctorale* of TCD MS 78 (ff. 130–77) contains an entry on Muicín under the guise of 'Mokyn'.[8] [p. 80, end of entry]

Add note: 8 *Colk.Cat.*, i, 122–5.

Add after **Araght**: **Arannán**. *See* Forannán of Alternan.

ARUIN

Add to note: 2 *EMH* 479 §203.

ATHRACHT of Killaraght

Add: The fragment, which was probably written by a Cistercian monk in the abbey of Boyle, establishes [p. 81, last line]

Add to note: 1 *BiblSS* ii, 576–8.

BAIRRE

Insert at start of chapter: **Bairre (Barra)** of Cork. *See* Fionnbharr of Cork.

BAIRRFHIONN of Aughkiletaun

Add: It has been suggested that he was the same as Moroc (from *Mobharróc) of the Scottish church of Dunblane, whose feast also fell on 8 November.[4] [p. 83, end of entry]

Add note: 4 *LegSS* 266–7, 399–400.

BAIRRFHIONN of Midíne

Add: An unpublished Office Life, compiled for the saint in his capacity as patron of the Waterford parish of Kilbarrymeaden, is preserved in a fourteenth-century manuscript in Corpus Christi College, Cambridge.[5] The saint's feast fell on 13 November.[6] [p. 84, end of entry]

Add notes: 5 *JCHAS* 58, 48; *MakS* 68n. 6 *MartG* 218.

BAODÁN of Cloney

Add: Glendalough.[10] He may also have been patron of Grange in the Dublin parish of Holmpatrick.[11] [p. 86, l. 22]

Add: on 13 December and perhaps also on 6 October.[12 13] [p. 86, l. 26]

Add (to) notes: 11 *IsPatrick* 54–5. [Renumber notes 11 and 12 to 12 and 13] ~~12~~ 13 *MartO²* 220, 251; *MartG* 190, 238; *MartD* 268, 334.

BAODÁN of Killoscobe

Add: commemorated on 23 March, at which date John Colgan also gave an account of him.[3] Baodán may have retained a connection with Munster through the church of Glenkeen in the Tipperary barony of Kilnamanagh Upper, which he surrendered, according to the Life of Fionnbharr, to the Cork saint.[3 4] [p. 87, end of entry]

Add (to) notes: **3** *ASH* 728. [Renumber note 3 to 4] **3 4** *BBa.* 68 §23.

BAOITHÍN of Ennisboyne
Read: **7** ~~AICW~~ *AICK*

BAOITHÍN of Iona

Read: his cult ~~is~~ are Taughboyne [p. 89, l. 20]

Add: Colum Cille, and Balrathboyne Glebe in the Meath parish of Balrathboyne, close to Kells, where a holy well also bears his name.[8] [p. 89, l. 21]

Add: Born, according to the Annals of Tighearnach in 536, Baoithín's obit [p. 89, l. 26]

Add to notes: **8** *OSL MH*, 43. **11** *ATig. s.a.*

BAOITHÍN of Taghboyne

Add: The notice in the Martyrology of Donegal states that he was also patron of Tibohine (Teach Baoithín) in the Roscommon barony of Frenchpark.[8] As such, he may also be the Baoithín remembered in the Mayo parish name of Crossboyne (Cros Bhaoithín), and perhaps also the saint of the name invoked in a poem by Donnchadh Mór Ó Dálaigh (†1244).[9] [p. 90, end of entry]

Add (to) notes: **8** *MartD* 52. **9** *DDé* 50; cf. *LME* vii, 251–4.

Add after **Basar**: **Beacon**. *See* Beagán

BEAG son of Dé Draoi

Add: According to the annals, he died in 553 (or 558).[8] [p. 91, end of entry]

Add (to) notes: **1** *BLCat.* ii, 311. **8** *AU s.a.*

BEAG BILE

Add: Colmán, Cuán, and Connaidhil, alias Conán, who was remembered on 8 March at a place called 'Cnodair', near Assaroe, now possibly Knader in the Donegal parish of Kilbarron.[1] [p. 91, l. 4 of entry]

Add to note: **1** *ASH* 563; *HDGP* v, 186.

BEAGÁN of Toureen

Add: Further south, at Mullinavat in the Kilkenny [p. 94, l. 2]

BEAGNAD of Kilbegnet
Add to note: **1** *TNW* 1071–2.

BEARACH

Add: The saint's coarb was among the ecclesiastics entitled to be present at the inauguration of O'Connor as king of Connacht, and his crozier [p. 96, l. 20]

Add: Bells associated with the saint, now all lost, are attested for Kilbarry and Glendalough in Ireland and Kilberry in Scotland.[24] [p. 96, end of entry]

Add (to) notes: **23** *JRSAI* 2, 340; *MSPAG* 188. **24** *EMH* 482 §216; 488 §236; 494 §249.

BEARCHÁN of Castlehaven

Add: Local tradition maintained that Bearchán came from Spain, but a member of the Uí Ghiolla Mhichíl branch of the Corca Laoighdhe was known as his *fear ionaid*, 'representative'.[3] [p. 96, l. 9 of entry]

Add to note: **3** LGen. 677.7.

BEARCHÁN of Clonsast

Add: Bearchán, representing his church, is also among the saints said, tendentiously, to have owed tribute to Caillín of Fenagh.[16] [p. 97, end of entry]

Add note: **16** BFen. 286.

BEARCHÁN of Druim Dóithe

Add: Finally, he may have given name to Clonfert (Cluain Fearta Bearcháin) in the Kildare parish of Balraheen.[4] [p. 98, end of entry]

Add note: **4** CR 10, 137; HDGP v, 121, 150.

BEINÉAN of Kilbennan

Add: Beinéan's brother Ceitheach, who was commemorated on 16 June, apparently at Oran in the Roscommon parish of the same name, with [p. 100, l. 12 of entry]

Add: Mathona – of what seems to be Shankill in the Roscommon parish of the same name – who [p. 101, l. 11 of entry]

Add: At his church in Glin he may also have been known as Mac Luighne, a name used for one of those called upon to assist Seanán of Scattery.[21] [p. 102, end of entry]

Add (to) notes: **2** BP 1185–91; VT 106; Mart T 50; MartG 116; MartD 170. **7** BP 1091–4; VT 8; Ainm 6, 26. **15** Ériu 45, 12 §8. **20** FL 80–1. **21** ZCP 10, 26 §22.

BEOAIDH of Ardcarn

Add: Beoaidh (anglicized Hugh) son of Olga [p. 103, l. 3 of entry]

Add: is still frequented and, according to John Colgan, the saint's bell, known as *Ceolán Beoaidh*, was kept at the church of Ballinagleragh in the same Leitrim parish.[5] [p. 103, l. 14 of entry]

Add: His coarb was among the ecclesiastics entitled to be present at the inauguration of O'Connor as king of Connacht.[7] [p. 103, end of entry]

Add (to) notes: **4** Breifne 4, 207. **5** ASH 563; EMH 478 §201. **7** JRSAI 2, 340; MSPAG 189.

BEOÁN of Meenan

Add to note: **6** LegSS 250–1, 326–7.

BIGSEACH of Kilbixy

Add: and, at 4 October, a glossator of the Martyrology of Óengus identified her with an otherwise unattested Balbina.[4] [p. 106, end of entry]

Add to note: **4** MartO 220.

BLÁN

Add to note: **2** LegSS 180–91, 328–30.

BLATHMHAC of Rath

Add to note: **6** SAM 24.1, 17, 20.

BRANNAMH of Tynagh
Add to note: 1 *Ainm* 1, 23–40.

BREACÁN of Inishmore
Add: Elsewhere in Galway, at Kilbrickan in the parish of Kilcummin, a healing stone was named Leac Bhreacáin after him.[10] A well was dedicated to him at Toomullin in the Clare parish of Killilagh.[11] [p. 113, end of entry]
Add notes: 10 *JGAHS* 64, 6. 11 *ACoC* 102.

BRÉANAINN
Add to note: 1 *CI* i, 103n.

BRÉANAINN of Birr
Read: closely associated, and a separate text maintains that he was owed a fee by the Uí Mhaine, whose territory later corresponded to the diocese of Clonfert.[3] [p. 114, l. 9 of entry]
Add to note: 3 *TEAB* 148 §§5–6.

BRÉANAINN of Clonfert
Add: build a church, a possible reference to Ogulla, whose patron was entitled to be present at O'Connor's inauguration.[11] [p. 116, l. 20]
Add: founding of Clonfert (in 558, according to the annals), perhaps [p. 116, l. 30]
Add: Commutations, and a Law named after him was proclaimed in Connacht in 744.[18] [p. 117, l. 2]
Add: Cannaway, Kilbrenan, parish of Moviddy, in the Cork barony of East Muskerry, and Kilmoe in the barony of West Carbery [p. 117, l. 4]
Add: Adhamhnán's reliquary, and a late medieval poem brings the saint to Greece and Rome, among other places.[26] Devotion to the saint was widespread on the Continent and, by the ninth century, a relic had arguably reached either Ferrières in France or the Rhineland.[27] [p. 117, l. last two lines of entry] [Renumber notes 27 and 28 to 28 and 29]
Add (to) notes: 5 *TEAB* 732–3. 6 *StH* 37, 9–26. 11 *JRSAI* 2, 340. 15 *AU* s.a. 18 *AU* s.a. 19 *AnH* 29, 8 §25. 26 *Éigse* 13, 92–8. 27 *SIHI* 10–15; *EIRD* 55–68; *RIW* 15–19.

BRÍGH of Barragh
Add: A print on the base of a font outside the doorway of the medieval church of Barragh is now known as 'St Patrick's footprint'.[4] [p. 117, end of entry]
Add note: 4 *RIGI* 235.

BRIGHID of Kildare
Add: Magh Aoi (Rathcroghan), where her coarb (in Ballintober) was later entitled to be present at O'Connor's inauguration.[8] [p. 123, l. 34 of entry]
Add: her cult which, while centred in Leinster, including Dublin, where churches in the ancient town centre, in Killester and Stillorgan preserved her memory, even reached [p. 124, l. 24]
Add: Adamhnán's reliquary and bells associate with her are attested for Kildare, Croaghpatrick and Beckery, parish of Glastonbury, Somerset, England.[23] [p. 125, l. 7]
Add: age of seventy (elsewhere given as eighty-eight), [p. 125, l. 12]

Add: A relic of the saint, accompanied by relics of her successor Darlughdhach and her bishop Conlaodh, had reached Saint-Maurice d'Agaune in the Swiss canton of Valais by 700, and by the mid-ninth century another relic is attested for the Rhineland.[29] [p. 125, end of entry]

Add (to) notes: **1** *Ériu* 54, 82–92; *BiblSS* iii, 430–7; *SBK* 81–93; *Peritia* 21, 192–6. **5** *SBK* 111–221. **8** *JRSAI* 2, 340. **10** *ZCP* 19, 120 §13. **14** *SBK* 168; *Keimelia* 519; *AH* 8, 15. **23** *EMH* 477 §197, 480 §207, 512 §292. **26** *MSNAF* 139; *EIRD* 55–68. **29** *RIW* 12–13, 15–19, 31.

BRIÚINSEACH
Add: A note added to Ó Cléirigh's index of the Martyrology of Donegal asks whether she is to be identified with Berriona/Buryan in Cornwall.[3] [p. 126, end of entry]

Add note: **3** *MartD* 368; cf. *SCorn.* 78.

Add after **Broinnfhinn**: Bromana. *See* Brónach of Kilbroney.

BRÓN
Add/read: Killaspugbrone.[3] ~~Bron's~~ Brón died, according to the annals, in 512, and his feast [p. 129, l. 12 of entry]

Add to note: **4** *AU s.a.*

BRÓNACH of Kilbroney
Add: Inghean Mhíolchon and, in Latin, Bromana) is said [p. 129, l. 3 of entry]

Add to notes: **1** *EA* 115–16, 309. **4** *EA* 114–16, 315.

BUADÁN
Add to notes: **2** *AnH* 12, 85. **5** *EMH* 392 §87.

BUITHE
Add to note: **13** *CL* 74–86.

CADÁN of Tamlaght-Ard
Add to note: **3** *AnH* 12, 82, 108, 110.

CAILLÍN
Add: his so-called, lately burnt, bell.[15] [p. 136, l. 10]
Add: They were also among the ecclesiastics entitled to be present at the inauguration of O'Connor as king of Connacht.[18] [p. 136, end of entry]

Add (to) notes: **4** *IML* 49–73. **15** *EMH* 452–5 §150. **18** *JRSAI* 2, 340; *MSPAG* 189.

CAIMÍN of Inishcaltra
Add: and Uí Bhriúin Rátha of the barony of Clare in south Connacht [p. 136, l. 7 of entry]
Add: Inishcaltra on which they remained for seven years, according to Colum's Life.[6] [p. 137, l. 6]
Add: monk.[9] The form Mochamóg is also used to describe him as one of Ireland's three noted *athlaoich* (former laymen).[10] [p. 137, l. 19] [Renumber notes 10–12 to 11–13]
Add: [New paragraph] Patron of Kilcaimin in the parish of Ballinacourty, barony of Dunkellin in south Galway, and dedicatee of a burial ground at Ballykinvarga in the Clare parish of Kilfenora, Caimín may [p. 137, l. 20]

Add: Martyrology of Usuard and the martyrology of the Regensburg Schottenkloster.[12] In 1607, Pope Paul V granted a plenary indulgence to pilgrims to Inishcaltra, and two years later thousands are reported to have been on the island during the week before Easter, which presumably coincided with the saint's feastday.[13] [p. 137, l. 24]

Add (to) notes: **3** *ILL* 358, 363. **6** *VSHH* 233 §30. **8** *SAM* 24.1, 17, 20. **10** *Anecd.* iii, 60. **11** *AIOY* §773. **12** *MartR* 48–9; *FSHIM* 236. **13** *AH* 3, 263; *PilgI* 54. **14** *NMAJ* 59, 13–29.

Cainneach of Aghaboe
Add: Colum Cille, with whom he is said to have exchanged poems of praise, and Comhghall of Bangor, [p. 139, l. 25]
Add: born in 516 or 527, and [p. 139, second last line of page]
Add: Constance and a relic of his reached the Continent, arguably either at Ferrières in France or some church in the Rhineland.[19] [p. 140, l. 5]
Add: saint and short office lessons in commemoration of him have been preserved in the Breviary of Aberdeen.[24] [p. 140, end of entry]

Add to notes: **1** *OLL* 1, 19–20. **9** *IMN* 3, 76. **13** *ACL* iii, 217–21. **16** *AnH* 12, 82–3, 107–10. **19** *EIRD* 55–68. **24** *LegSS* 243–5, 369–70.

Add after **Cainneach** of Drumud: **Cainneach** of Magherintemple, parish of Drung, barony of Tullygarvey, Co. Cavan. Since this bearer of the name shared a dedication with 'Columba', he is likely to have been identical with Cainneach of Aghaboe.[1]

1 *Breifne* 4, 202; *CPL* 6, 153.

Cainnear of Rinn Allaidh
Add to note: **2** *LegSS* 252–4, 368–9.

Cairbre Crom
Add to note: **3** *TEAB* 465–73.

Cairbre Oilithir
Add to note: **2** *TNW* 1078.

Cairneach
Add: at Dulane, where he had already allegedly reburied Niall Naoighiallach, ancestral king of the Uí Néill, and a poem [p. 145, l. 27 of entry]
Add: Law of Adhamhnán, and, in addition to being named with Beinéan and Patrick among those chosen to arrange the *Seanchas Mór*, a *codach*, 'covenant', arranged by him between Muircheartach son of Earc and the Cianachta is also attested.[15] [p. 146, end of entry]

Add to notes: **6** *MartO²* 246. **15** *Ériu* 45, 12 §8, 25 §8.2; *IrT* iii, 5 §14.

Caoide of Donaghedy
Add to note: **3** *EMH* 484 §223.

Caoimhghin
Add: who is said by the annalists to have died at the ~~advanced~~ age of 120 [p. 148, last line]
Add: Caoimhghín's relics, which, presumably enshrined, were taken on tour in 790 together with those of Crónán of Clondalkin, was a bell named *Bobán*, which

was again used to bind an agreement between two twelfth-century kings.²⁶ Relics of the saint also found their way to the Continent, among other places to Sens and, arguably, either Ferrières in France or somewhere in the Rhineland.²⁷ The saint was patron of the secular families of Uí Thuathail (O'Tooles) and Uí Bhroin (Byrnes).²⁸ [p. 150, end of entry]

Add (to) notes: **8** cf. *BLCat*. i, 637–8. **22** *AU/ATig. s.a.* cf. *CI* i, 130n. **26** *AU s.a.*; *EMH* 488 §235; *AClon*. 1139. **27** *MSNAF* 138; *EIRD* 55–68; *RIW* 15–19. **28** *FFÉ* iii, 112.

CAOIREACH DHEARGÁIN
Add: her as a sister of Brughach [p. 151, l. 1]
Add: on 9 February, and one set of annals places her death in 579.⁸ [p. 151, end of entry]

Add (to) note: **8** *CS s.a*

CAOLAINN
Add: litany of virgins, and she is one of four female saints invoked in a poem by Donnchadh Mór Ó Dálaigh (†1244).⁹
Add: on this day.¹¹ The saint's monument was located at Ulaidh Caolainn in the Mayo barony of Carra.¹²

Add (to) notes: **3** *Celtica* 32, 115. **5** *OFWC* 103–4. **9** *DDé* 50. **10** *OFWC* 104. **12** *LGen*. 271.6.

Add after **Caolán of Annaghkeelaun**: **Caolán** of Inishcaltra. *See* Caolán of Youghalarra

CAOLÁN of Nendrum
Add/read: other saints, ~~including~~ notably those of Colmán of Dromore and Finnian of Movilla, both of whom he is said to have tutored, as well as from the Tripartite Life. [p. 153, l. 8]
Add: Finally, a synchronistic poem on emperors and kings assigns Mochaoi to a church named Cluain Cha, possibly the same as Clonca in the Donegal barony of Inishowen, and also provides him with a descent from Lughaidh Lágha.¹³ [p. 153, end of entry]

Add (to) notes: **4** *VSHH* 357–8 §3; *EA* 189; *ASH* 438. **11** cf. *CI* i, 144n. **13** *Peritia* 22–3, 116 §20.

CAOLÁN of Youghalarra
Add: on 29 July, who is credited with having written in verse Brighid of Kildare's sixth Life.⁴ [p. 154, l. 1]

Add to note: **4** *ASH* 592, 596–8.

CAOMHÁN of Anatrim
Add: From Aran the cult may have spread to the island of Inishglora, off the Mayo coast, on which an otherwise unattested Mochaomhóg is said to have befriended and subsequently baptized the celebrated 'Children of Lir'.¹⁰ [p. 155, end of entry]

Add note: **10** *OCL* 31 §58, 72.

CAOMHÁN BREAC of Russagh
Read: and obit (~~625~~ 615) assigned [p. 156, l. 7]

CAOMHÁN SANTLEATHAN
Add to note: **9** *TNW* 1079–83.

CAOMHLACH
Read: *Audite bonum exemplum* which some scholars take to have been written by
Colmán Eala.[3] [p. 157, last line]

Add to note: **3** *PSP* 41–5; *IIAM* 563–4.

Add after **Cassidus: Cathal** of Ballycahill, barony of Eliogarty, Co. Tipperary. A
reinterpretation of the name Bealach Achaille (way of Achall) as Baile Cathail
(Cathal's place) led to the mistaken assumption, already attested in the early
seventeenth century, that the place was named after Cataldo, patron of Taranto
in southern Italy, who was traditionally, but wrongly, regarded as an Irishman.[1]
Cathal also came to be venerated in the Tipperary parish of Shanrahan, barony
of Iffa and Offa West.[2]

Add notes: **1** *ASH* 544 §2; *PCNT* 315; *HDGP* ii, 100; *SacH* 355–63. **2** *ASH* 544–5; *SacH* 356.

CEALLACH of Armagh
Add: Germany in the ~~later~~ middle of the twelfth century [p. 161, second last line
of entry]

CEALLACH of Killala
Add: Ceallach son of Connmhach is also among those invoked in a poem calling
on saints to assist Seanán of Scattery.[6] [p. 162, l. 2]

Add note: **6** *ZCP* 10, 26 §21.

CEALLACHÁN
Read: barony of ~~Dartree~~ Cremorne, Co. Monaghan, [p. 161, l. 1 of entry]
Add: Ballyoughtera, probably recorded corruptly as 'Martre Chalwallin', was [p.
162, l. 11 of entry]
Add: Cloyne, 'Ceallachán's burial-place' in the Pipe Roll of Cloyne, but no
feastday [p. 162, end of entry]

Add to note: **4** *PRC* 10, 169.

CEARC of Tulach
Add: The saint's name may be preserved in the townland name Ardkirk, parish
of Donaghmoyne, on Monaghan's boundary with Louth.[4] [p. 165, l. 2]

Add note: **4** *ClRec.* 20, 580.

CEASÁN
Add to note: **6** *LegSS* 76–9.

Add after **Céirseach: Ceitheach** of Oran. *See* Beinéan of Kilbennan.

Add after **Christianus: Cian** of Knockeyon (Cnoc Céin?), parish of Faughalstown,
barony of Fore, Co. Westmeath. Situated on the hill of Knockeyon was an
'ancient chapel' dedicated, according to Sir Henry Piers in 1682, to a saint named
'Eyen or Keyen'.[1] According to the same authority a pilgrimage was made to the
site on the first Sunday in harvest, and this reference to the beginning of August
is corroborated in other accounts.[2] As Cian was the father of Lugh, whence
Lughnasa (*Lúnasa*), the Irish name for August, the saint so-named is probably
intended by the form 'Keyen'. Also on this hill, near the pilgrimage site, was

'St Coragh's or Coiragh's Well', named after an abbot of Kells in Co. Kilkenny who, having sinned with a woman, retired to the hill as a hermit.[3] This man's name may reflect the Irish form Cobhuir (Cobhrach?). A saint of the name Cobhuir was remembered on 30 July, and again, under the diminutive guise of Cobhrán, on 2 August.[4]

Add notes: **1** FL 132; OSL WH ii, 289. **2** OSL WH ii, 294; FL 133. **3** FL 133. **4** MartT 59; MartG 146, 148; MartD 204, 208.

CIANÁN

Add: Law of Adhamhnán, and his name is also invoked in a poem attributed to Moling.[9] [p. 167, l. 1]

Add: a contemporary of Patrick, and his body reputedly remained incorrupt over at least five hundred years after his death.[13] [p. 167, l. 8]

Add to notes: **9** Anecd. ii, 28 §1. **13** WBP 62 §15.

CIAR of Kilkeary

Add: 16 October, the second of which may have been influenced by the presence of an African saint named Caera in the Roman list of the day.[4] [p. 167, l. 10 of entry]

Add: Ciar died, according to the annals, in 681.[10] [p. 168, end of entry]

Add (to) notes: **4** Ainm 3, 3. **10** ATig s.a. 680.

CIARÁN of Castlekeeran

Add: His feast was celebrated on 14 June, and two days earlier according to the Martyrology of Turin, which may reflect practice at the church of Templekeeran in the Meath barony of Skreen.[6] He may also have been patron of the adjoining parish of Munterconnaught in the Cavan barony of Castlerahan.[7] Finally, since the parish named after him is separated by one parish only from that of Teltown, he may well be the Ciarán named as one of three saintly guarantors of the famous assembly held in the latter parish.[8] [p. 169, end of entry]

Add (to) notes: **6** FIM 128–9. **7** Breifne 4, 203. **8** MD iv, 158.

CIARÁN of Clonmacnoise

Add: belonging to Armagh, but the same author states that Ciarán was baptized by a disciple of Patrick named Iustus who had previously baptized the people of Uí Mhaine.[17] [p. 170, l. 27]

Add: John the Apostle, and such was the spread of devotion to him that other saints are said to have brought about his early death by fasting against him.[20] [p. 170, l. 33]

Add: Ciarán's Law (cáin), which had previously been proclaimed in Connacht in 744, 788 and 814.[30] [p. 171, l. 11]

Add: Relics of the saint also found their way to the Continent, among other places to Sens and, arguably, either Ferrières in France or the Rhineland.[33] Finally, his coarb at Aghkeran in the Roscommon parish of Fuerty was among those entitled to be present at the inauguration of the king of Connacht.[34] [p. 171, end of entry]

Add (to) notes: **5** LisL 3989. **14** AClon. 82. **17** 146 §28.24. **18** TromG 1282–4. **20** AB 69, 104; Éigse 2, 183–6. **21** cf. AU s.a. 512. **24** OFWC 97. **30** AU s.a. **31** EMH 481 §212. **33** MNSAF 138; EIRD 55–68; RIW 15–19. **34** MSPAG 189.

CIARÁN of Seirkieran

Add: who allegedly gave instructions, which included the sound of a bell, up to then mute, as to where Ciarán should position his church, [p. 172, l. 27 of entry]
Add: as abbot and, according to John O'Donovan, in his time the saint was still venerated throughout the diocese of Ossory where people swore 'by his hand, *dar láimh Chiaráin*, and by his name, corrupted to *Parán*'.[20] [p. 173, end of entry]

Add to notes: **8** EMH 480 §211. **20** UL Camb. Add. 622 (1, 2) 25.

CIARÁN of Tubbrid

Read: the martyrologies, including one kept in the Regensburg *Schottenkloster*, commemorate him on 10 November.[7] [p. 174, l. 11]

Add to note: **7** FSHIM 242; MartR 161.

Add after **Cneas**: **Cobhair (Cobhrán, Cobhrach?)**. *See* Cian of Knockeyen.

COGA

Add: she appears to have given name to Kilcoke in the Laois parish of Rathdowney, to Kilcoke in the Tipperary parish of Loughmoe East, and to Kilcock in the Roscommon parish of Kilmore,

Add to note: **4** CLTÁ 95.

COINCHEANN of Killagh Abbey
Read at note: **1** CGSH §7410.1 §410.1.

COIREALL of Clonkeenkerrill
Read: in Sligo, now possibly Tawnagh in the parish of Kilshalvy.[5] [p. 181, l. 6]

Add to note: **5** DEPPP 343.

COLGA of Clonmacnoise
Add: He has also been identified with the Colga whose opinions are cited in the ninth-century text known as *The Monastery of Tallaght*.[3] [p. 182, end of entry]

Add note: **3** MT §56, 65, 81, p. 178.

COLMÁN of Cloyne
Read: the descendants of ~~a southern king, Lughaidh Lágha~~ Aonghas Catta, eponym of a rent-paying people called Catraighe.[5] [p. 185, l. 18]
Add: attributed to Colmán, and a late (?) tract preserved in the *Leabhar Muimhneach* refers to tribute due to him and his church from every king of Cashel.[12] [p. 186, l. 5]
Add: Born, according to the Annals of Inisfallen, in 528, Colmán died, according to the same source, in 606.[16] [p. 186, end of entry]

Add (to) notes: **1** HMDC 5–8. **4** LM 90. **12** LM 90; cf. AB 66, 202–4. **16** AI s.a.

COLMÁN of Dromore
Add: A full office Life of the saint, similar to that in the *Codex Salmanticensis*, is preserved in the Breviary of Aberdeen.[14] In Scotland, he was patron of the church of Inchmahome, Perthshire.[15] [p. 188, end of entry]

Add (to) notes: **1** SGS 24, 253–65. **14** LegSS 124–9, 327–9. **15** SGS 24, 263.

COLMÁN of Inishbofin
Add: In Ireland, in 668, according to the annals, Colmán founded a church on Inishbofin, [p. 190, l. 14 of entry]
Add: on 13 November, unless this related to his namesake, Colmán Lobhar of Moynoe.[6] [p. 190, l. 24 of entry]
Add: An Office Life, preserved in the Breviary of Aberdeen, assigns his feast to 18 February, thus confusing him with Colmán of Moray.[7] His coarb at Mayo was among the ecclesiastics present at the inauguration of O'Connor as king of Connacht.[8] [p. 190, end of entry]

Add (to) notes: **2** *AU s.a.* **7** *LegSS* 58–61, 336–7. **8** *JRSAI* 2, 340.

Add before **Colmán** of Kilcolman, Co. Limerick: **Colmán** of Kilclonfert. *See* Colmán of Templeshanbo.

COLMÁN of Kilmacduagh
Add to note: **2** cf. *BLCat.* i, 638.

COLMÁN of Kilroot
Read: his namesake of both Holdenstown (Bealach Buaidhghe) and Clara – which adjoins Tiscoffin (*Teach Scoithín*), the house of Scoithín of the family of Ailbhe – in the same county.[5] [p. 194, last two lines of entry]

Add before **Colmán** of Linns: **Colmán** of Lindisfarne *see* **Colmán** of Inishboffin.

COLMÁN of Linns
Add to note: **4** *JCLAS* 28, 22–3.

COLMÁN of Moray
Add to note: **3** *LegSS* 336–7.

COLMÁN of Myshall
Add: Finally, in the guise of Colum, alias Colum Crosaire, the saint is said to have been left in Donaghmore by Patrick, who reputedly founded the church.[8]

Add note: **8** *BP* 1980–2 (= *VT* 170); *HDGP* vii, 121–2.

COLMÁN of Templeshanbo
Add to note: **7** *MartO* 198.

COLMÁN CEARR
Read: his church – now ~~possibly Allstonekill in the townland of Whitegate~~ probably in the townland of Meelick – on the edge of Lough Derg, [p. 202, ll 3–4 of entry]

COLMÁN CÚILE
Add: and he may also have been remembered on 6 October.[4] [p. 203, end of entry]
Add to note: **4** *MartO*¹ 154–5.

COLMÁN EALA
Add: much debate, as is his possible authorship of *Audite omnes amantes*, an early hymn in honour of St Patrick which is also attributed to Secundinus (Seachnall).[22] [p. 205, l. 11]

Read: an encounter with ~~Patrick~~ Caoilte of the Fianna at 'Loch an Daimh Dheirg', [p. 205, l. 16]

Add: Lynn near Mullingar (a place allegedly cursed by the saint), and Conry [p. 205, l. 22]

Add: died in 611 at the age of 55, [p. 205, l. 31]

Add: from a horse.[31] Within Leinster, Colmán was also venerated at Tullaghanbrogue in the Kilkenny baronies of Crannagh and Shillelogher.[32] [p. 205, end of entry]

Add (to) notes: **22** PSP 40–6; IIAM 562–3. **26** MartD 384. **30** AU/ATig. s.a. **32** HADO iii, 385.

COLMÁN IOMRAMHA of Inishmore

Add: According to the Annals of Inisfallen, he died in 751.[4] [p. 206, end of entry]

Add note: **4** AI s.a.

Add after **Colmán Iomramha** of Inishmore: **Colmán** of Kilclooney in the Armagh barony of Fews Lower. Of this saint very little is known. It has been shown, however, that he is found in early documents as Colmán of the Maca Coirtchidh and, as such, he figures in the martyrological lists for 18 October, which describe him as an abbot.[1] The lists of homonymous saints also include his name.[2]

Add notes: **1** SAM 2.1, 163–5; MartT 81; MartG 198; MartD 278. **2.** CGSH 143 (§707.233).

COLMÁN LOBHAR

Add: Colmán may also have been remembered on 13 November, unless Magh Eó in this case refers to Mayo.[4] [p. 206, end of entry]

Add note: **4** MartG 218; MartD 308.

Add after **Colum** of Culbrim: **Colum** of Donaghmore. *See* Colmán of Myshall.

COLUM of Terryglass

Read: Lough Derg ~~including~~ before arriving at Inishcaltra [p. 210, l. 18]

Read: venerated ~~before finally settling in Terryglass~~. Though most of the remainder of his life was spent on an island in the Shannon estuary, near Canon Island, the saint's remains were eventually brought to Terryglass and buried there. [New paragraph] Among the many [p. 210, l. 20]

Read: likened in manners to ~~James the Apostle~~ the apostle and evangelist Matthew.[13] [p. 210, l. 41]

Add to/read notes: **12** Cf. VSHH 232 §28. **13** ~~CGSH §712.11~~ CGSH §712.10

COLUM CILLE

Add: out of Fanad and, similarly, in the poem addressed to Baoithín in which more portents of the end of the world are outlined.[32] [p. 214, l. 9]

Add: Many relics of the saint found their way to the Continent, among other places to Sens and, arguably, either to Ferrières in France or to some church in the Rhineland.[38] A relic of the saint, accompanied by relics of Adhamhnán and Finnian of Movilla, had also reached Saint-Maurice d'Agaune in the Swiss canton of Valais by the second half of the eighth century.[39] [p. 214, end of entry]

Add (to) notes: **25** AmraeCC 77–157; **32** TEAB 690 §1; 697–704. **35** PRIA 98C1, 4–5. **38** SIHI 63–70; MSNAF 449; EIRD 55–68; RIW 15–19. **39** RIW 13, 32.

COMÁN OF ROSCOMMON

Add: His coarb was among the ecclesiastics entitled to be present at the inauguration of O'Connor as king of Connacht.[14] [p. 217, end of entry]

Add note: **14** *MSPAG* 189.

COMHGHALL OF BANGOR

Add: barony of Idrone (Uí Dhróna), and further north in Leinster, he was patron of Clontarf in the Dublin barony of Coolock, until replaced by John the Baptist.[15] [p. 218, last line]

Add: his obit is placed ~~in the annals~~ at 601–2, with one set of annals claiming that he was ninety.[21] [p. 219, l. 12]

Add: The saint's relics, subsequently taken for safety to Antrim, were removed violently from their shrine in Bangor in 824, and his staff was left to the 'Foreigners' after the battle of Downpatrick in 1178.[24] Relics of the saint also found their way to the Continent, among other places to the Rhineland, Sens and, arguably, Ferrières in France.[25] [p. 219, ll 17–18] [Renumber note 25 to 26]

Add: His name is invoked in both Stowe Missal litanies, and office lessons commemorating the saint are preserved in the Breviary of Aberdeen.[~~25~~ 26] [p. 219, end of entry]

Add (to) notes: **13** *CM* 52. **15** *SacH* 41 §48. **16** *AnH* 12, 108, 111. **21** *AnH* 12, 108, 111. **25** *MSNAF* 59, 138; *EIRD* 55–68, *RIW* 16–19. **~~25~~ 26** *LegSS* 120–3, 344–5.

COMHGHALL of Carrowmore

Add to note: **6** *Mdub.* 18, 153.

COMHGHÁN of Cluain Connaidh

Add to note: **5** *LegSS* 245–7, 345–6.

COMHGHÁN of Killeshin

Add: Comhghán of the Maca Teimhne died, according to the annals, in 664.[11] [p. 221, end of entry]

Add note: **11** *AU s.a.*

COMNAID

Read: in honour of 'Cumenod' (also written Commaneth).[1] [p. 221, l. 3 of entry]

Add to note: **1** *ACE* 264.

CONALL of Drumcliff

Read: The Conall venerated at ~~(Sherkin)~~ Tullagh in the Cork barony [p. 222, l. 24 of entry]

Add to note: **3** *SAM* 24.1, 20.

CONALL of Inishkeel

Add: parish of Inishkeel, and his 'healing stone' was kept at Bruckless in the parish of Killaghtee.[4] [p. 223, l. 6 of entry]

Add to notes: **4** *JGAHS* 64, 5. **7** *EMH* 317–22 §8. **8** *AnH* 12, 81, 108, 110.

Add before **Conbhran**: **Conán** son of Tighearnach. *See* Beag Bile.

Add after **Conbhran**: **Connla**. *See* Conlaodh.

CONLAODH CRÁIBHTHEACH
Add: Conlaodh (alias Con(n)la, anglicized Conleth), [p. 223, l. 3 of entry]
Add: He is said to have died in 520 and hHis remains [p. 224, l. 19]
Add: A relic of the saint, accompanied by relics of Brighid and her successor Darlughdhach, had reached Saint-Maurice d'Agaune in the Swiss canton of Valais by 700.[11] [p. 224, end of entry]

Add (to) notes: **10** AU s.a. **11** RIW 12–13, 31.

Add after **Connaidhil** son of Síolán: **Connaidhil** son of Tighearnach. *See* Beag Bile.

CORMAC of Durrow
Add: He is said to have formed a union (*aonta*) with Moling of St Mullins.[10] [p. 226, end of entry]

Add (to) notes: **8** TNW 1090–1. **10** Anecd. ii, 28 §2.

CORMAC of Killala
Read: he is said to have assisted in the birth of Aodhán son of Gabhrán (d. 606), king of Scotland, and to have foretold the births [p. 227, l. 11]

Add to note: **3** IrT iii, 3 §8, 4 §9; 4–5 §11.

CORMAC son of Eachaidh
Add: Cormac's Well at Altamuskin in the Tyrone parish of Errigal Keerogue may also have taken its name from the saint.[4] [p. 228, l. 8]

Add note: **4** TEHS 548.

CRÁNAID
Add to note: **2** HMDC 11–12.

CRÉADH
Add: 'Kilcreddy' in the Kilkenny parish of Derrynahinch, of which Brighid was believed to be patron, has also been taken to represent 'Crede's church'.[3] [p. 229, end of entry]

Add note: **3** HADO iv, 18–19.

CRÍODÁN of Kilcredaun
Add to note: **2** CKV 60.

Add before **Crónán** of Carran: **Crónán** of Balla. *See* Mochua of Balla.

CRÓNÁN of Clashmore
Add: Meallán, and this patronymic is repeated in the Life of Mochuda, which includes him among the twelve disciples of the Lismore saint.[1] [p. 233, l. 5 of entry]
Read: Located south of Swords by one glossator, ~~the Meath church … his father Meallán~~ 'Glashmore Abbey' in the townland of Mooretown, parish of Swords, where there is a holy well dedicated to the saint, may be intended.[4] [p. 233, ll 14–15]

Add to notes: **1** VSHP I, 182 §34. **2** ASH 589. **3** Rep. Nov. 2, 81; AHWD 12, 42.
Renumber note: **6** to **5**.

CRÓNÁN of Clondalkin
Add to notes: **1** *Seanchas* 182–4. **5** *AfL* 31, 36.

CRÓNÁN of Roscrea
Add: Uí Chearbhaill (O'Carrolls) and Uí Mheachair (Mahers) of Éile, [p. 234, l. 3 of entry]
Add: Crónán's coarb was entitled to a horse and garment from every chieftain of the Uí Mheachair of Éile, as well as a place of honour at the chieftain's inauguration.[19] [p. 235, end of entry]
Add (to) notes: **1** *OCBG* §2046. **19** *OCBG* §2046.

CRÓNÁN of Tomgraney
Add to notes: **2** *NL* 169–70. **5** *NL* 168–70. **6** *CGSH* §707.515. **8** *SAM* 24.1, 17, 19.

Add ahead of **Crónán Sapiens:** **Crónán Luachra.** *See* Mochua Luachra.

CRUACHÁN
Add to note: **5** *IMN* 3, 77–8.

CRUITHNEACHÁN
Add: An early seventeenth-century description of the diocese of Derry renders his name as *Chronicanus.*[6] [p. 238, end of entry]
Add note: **6** *AnH* 12, 108, 111.

CUÁN of Airbhre
Add: 3 February, but this man's name has recently been identified as Comhghán.[4] [p. 239, l. 11 of entry]
Add to note: **4** *TNW* 1094

CUANA of Eonish
Add: **Cuana** of Eóinis, now either White Island or Davy's Island on Lough Erne, in the parish of Magheraculmoney, barony of Lurg, Co. Fermanagh.[1] According to his pedigree, [p. 240, start of entry] [Renumber notes 1–5 as 2–6]
Read: anachoritic life on ~~Eoinish~~ Eóinis and [p. 240, l. 4 of entry]
Add (to) note: **1** *Peritia* 16, 477–8; *FHHS* 576.

CUANA of Kilcoona
Add to note: **13** *EMH* 450–2 §149.

CUANA ÓGH
Add: Cuana of Ros Eó died in 721.[5] [p. 242, end of entry]
Add note: **5** *AU s.a.*

Add before **Cuimín:** **Cuculanus.** See Cúlán. **Cuddy.** *See* Mochuda.

CUIMÍN FADA of Clonfert
Add: according to the annals, which date his birth, however, to 592.[6] [p. 244, l. 16]
Add: Celebra Iuda, the famous paschal letter attributed to Cummian, and some [p. 244, l. 25]
Add: Born in 590 or 592, the saint died, according to the annals, in 662, and h~~H~~is feastday fell [p. 244, l. 40]

Add: of the *moralia*.[14] Under the guise of Sean-Chuimín, he was invoked with Bréanainn in a poem by Donnchadh Mór Ó Dálaigh.[15] His remains [p. 244, l. 44] [Renumber note 15 to 16]

Add (to) notes: **1** *IIAM* 583–7. **8** *CLCP* 7–25; *IIAM* 577. **13** *AU s.a.* **15** *Dán Dé* 50.

CUIMÍN FADA of Kilcummin

Add: in violence, which may also have involved the bringing to Kilcomin (alias Díseart Cuimín) of the relics of Peter and Paul from where they subsequently 'escaped' back to Roscrea.[5] [p. 245, l. 18]

Add: At Kilcummin he was remembered as 'judge and arbitrator' in all disputes.[9] [p. 245, end of entry]

Add (to) notes: **5** *MartO* 78. **9** *JGAHS* 64, 7.

CÚLÁN

Add: (also written Cúiléan, as in Giolla Cúiléin of the Éile, [p. 246, l. 23]

Add: In the Catalogue of the principal Irish saints, Cúlán's name became Cuculanus.[5] [p. 247, end of entry]

Add (to) notes: **1** *CGH* 154a28. **5** *Seanchas* 410 §86; *FEMN* 355 (§153); cf. *HCIC* 49.

Add ahead of **Cunnlan**: **Cummian**. *See* Cuimín.

CURCACH of Kilcorkey

Read: of Kilcorkey, where ... July⁺ ... Greagraighe. Graveyard, townland of Knockbrandon Upper in the parish of Kilnahue.[2] [p. 249, ll 3–5]

Add to note: **2** *TNW* 1090

DAGHÁN of Ennereilly

Read: Daghán's death as ~~639~~ 641.[9] [p. 251, l. 32]

Add note: **9** *AU s.a.* 908 / *ATig. s.a.* 640.

DAIGH of Inishkeen

Add: the Life, which, although dated to the ninth century in a recent study, shows many signs of an Augustinian provenance.[3a] [p. 252, l. 16]

Add: died on 18 August ~~588~~ 587, [p. 253, l. 5]

Add note: **3a** *CHSC* 154–7.

DALLÁN FORGHAILL

Read: Magh Shléacht in the Cavan barony of ~~Tullyhunco~~ Tullyhaw [p. 255, l. 16]

Add: on 31 July, but more probably a still unidentified Maighean in Magh Shléacht in the Cavan parish of Templeport, adjoining Kildallan.[6] [p. 255, l. 23 of entry]

Add: son of Aodh, while a gloss added to a pedigree in the Book of Lecan attaches him to the Dál bhFiadach of north Down.[10] [p. 255, end of entry]

Add to notes: **6** *MD* iii, 396; *IIAM* 568. **10** *CGH* 330b10; cf. *IIAM* 567.

DAMHÁN of Feamore

Add to note: **2** but cf. *TNW* 1098–9.

DAMHÁN son of Daimhín

Add to note: **5** *Ainm* 3, 3.

DAMHNAD
Add: **Damhnad** of Caldavnet (Ceall Damhnadan), parish of Tedavnet
Add to notes: **2** *Ériu* 54, 80–1. **4** *IER* I ser. 7, 71; *DDSC* 19–20. **6** *IER* I ser. 7, 71.

DARLUGHDHACH of Kildare
Add: A relic of the saint, accompanied by relics of her predecessor Brighid and bishop Conlaodh of Kildare, had reached Saint-Maurice d'Agaune in the Swiss canton of Valais by 700.[6] [p. 258, end of entry]
Add (to) notes: **3** *LegSS* 391–2. **6** *RIW* 12–13, 31.

DÉAGLÁN
Add: local dynasty of the Déise, of which he was later patron.[3] [p. 258, l. 9 of entry]
Add to notes: **3** *FFÉ* iii, 112. **18** *EMH* 485 §225.

DEIRBHILEADH
Add: female saints, and she is the first of the female saints invoked in a poem by Donnchadh Mór Ó Dálaigh († 1244).[8] [p. 261, l. 23 of entry]
Add to notes: **8** *DDé* 50. **9** *AbEMLS* 101–5.

Add ahead of **Díoma** of Killagone: **Díoma** of Dorrha. *See* Modhíomóg of Glankeen.

DÍOMÁN of Clonkeen
Add: Kilkenny, possibly also the neighbouring parish of Kilmodum (from Cill Modhoma), and Coolhull in the Wexford parish of Bannow.[6] [p. 267, l. 10]

DÍORAIDH
Read: Díoraidh (Dirath) died as a bishop at Ferns in 693, [p. 267, l. 8 of entry]

DOCHONNA of Assylin
Read: Mochonna of Derry ~~a probable double of Colum Cille~~ who died, according to the annals, in 706.[6] [p. 269, last line]
Add to notes: **6** *AU* s.a. **7** *JRSAI* 2, 340.

DOCHUAILÉAN
Add to note: **3** *TEAB* 690 §3.

DODHRÁN
Read: the feast ~~may have been~~ was noticed in the martyrology kept in the Regensburg *Schottenkloster* and again, albeit under [p. 271, l. 1]
Add to notes: **2** *FSHIM* 242. **4** *SAM* 24.1, 17, 19–20

Add ahead of **Domhainghin** of Delgany: **Dolua**. *See* Molua

DOMHANGHART
Add: the saint (variously called Donard, Donnart and Donnaght, and latinized by Gerald of Wales as *Dominicus*) [p. 272, l. 11 of entry]
Add: Upper Iveagh, where relics of his, a bell known as *glúnán* and a shrine of the saint's 'shoe', ... on 24 March, but the pilgrimage to his church on Slieve Donard,

a *Lughnasa* celebration attended by thousands, was held on 25 July.[6] [p. 272, ll 14–15 of entry]

Add: However, according to the annals he died either in 466 or 507.[8] A short office Life of the saint was published by John Colgan.[9] [p. 272, end of entry]

Add (to) notes: **4** THEH 141. **5** ASH 743; EMH 469 §181. **6** FL 84–96. **8** AU s.a. **9** ASH 743.

DONNÁN of Eigg

Add: Donnán gave name to several churches in Scotland and, by the ninth century, a relic of his had reached the Continent, arguably at Ferrières in France or at some church in the Rhineland.[5] The saint's martyrdom became the subject of a tale, now lost, and some sources place the event on a rock (or island) named 'Aldasain / insula Alasina', now Ailsa Craig in the Firth of Clyde.[5 6] [Renumber note 5 as 6]

Add (to) notes: **5** LegSS 351; EIRD 55–68; RIW i 15–19. **5 6** Anecd. ii, 47 §8; CGSH §717; MartO² 114; FSHIM 236.

Add after **Donnán** of Eigg: **Donnán** of Hareisland, parish of Bunown, barony of Kilkenny West, Co. Westmeath. According to the Latin Life of Ciarán of Clonmacnoise, Hareisland was first occupied by its subject, who subsequently relinquished it to Donnán of the Corca Bhaiscinn of south-west Clare.[1] The much later vernacular Life of Ciarán states that Donnán was both the son of a brother of Seanán of Scattery, named Liath in *Genealogiae Regum et Sanctorum Hiberniae*, and a uterine brother of Seanán himself.[2] However, Donnán is not among those listed as children of Seanán's mother, either in the tract on the mothers of the saints or in a poem on Fíonmhaith daughter of Baoth.[3] Donnán was remembered on Hareisland in Lough Ree on 7 January.[4]

Add (to) notes: **1** VSHP i, 211 §28. **2** LisL 4361–2; GRSH 78. **3** CGSH §722.8; IrT iv, 93–4. **4** MartT 5; MartG 10; MartD 8.

DONNCHADH

Add: Dennis's well at Elm Park in the Dublin parish of Clontarf may also be called after him.[5] [p. 273, end of entry]

Add note: **5** AHWD 12.

Add before **Drugán**: **Dothearnóg**. *See* Earnán of Inis Caoin. **Drostán**. *See* Troscán.

DUBH DÚIN
Add to note: **3** AnH 12, 82, 108, 110.

DÚILEACH
Add to note: **1** AH 8, 20–1.

DÚNCHADH of Clonmacnoise
Add to note: **4** cf. MartD 404

DÚNCHADH of Iona
Add to note: **2** AU s.a.

ÉADAOIN
Add: Finally, Éadaoin, representing her church, is among those said tendentiously to have owed tribute to Caillín of Fenagh.[5] [p. 279, end of entry]

Add note: **5** BFen. 286.

Add after **Eagmhacht**: **Ealáir** of Monaincha (Loch Cré), parish of Corbally, barony of Ikerrin, Co. Tipperary. The church of Ealáir (Latin Hilarius) was located in an area later controlled by the Éile family of Uí Chearbhaill, which probably explains the saint's spurious Cianachta pedigree, preserved uniquely in *Genealogiae Regum et Sanctorum Hiberniae.*[1] Described as an anchorite and scribe, the saint is also named as an authority on *céile Dé* practice in 'The Monastery of Tallaght', a ninth-century treatise on the teaching of Maol Ruain and his disciples.[2] His place in the body of the list for 7 September is an indication of his inclusion in the Martyrology of Tallaght from the very beginning.[3] Ealáir 'of the Island' died in 807, and his feast fell on 7 September.[4]

Add notes: 1 GRSH 123 §11. 2 MT 128, 135. 3 MartT 69. 4 AU s.a.; MartT 69; MartG 172; MartD 238.

EALLÓG
Add: in the Wexford parish of Templetown and at Templeogue (from Teach Meallóg) in the Dublin parish of Tallaght.[3] [p. 280, l. 10]
Add to notes: 2 TNW 1069–71. 3 Ibid.; CECW 128–9, 206; HookP 25; AH 8, 30.

ÉANÁN of Drumraney
Add: Éanán is said to have died in 633, and he was remembered [p. 280, l. 25]
Add to notes: 3 ILL 269. 8 ATig. s.a. 632.

ÉANÁN of Glenealy
Add: **Éanán** of Glenealy and Rosminogue. *See* Méanóg.

ÉANNA of Inishmore
Read: Creamhthainn, a people settled ~~further north within the diocese of Clogher (Oirghialla)~~ in the Meath barony of Slane.[4] [p. 281, l. 15 of entry]
Add to note: 20 SAM 24.1, 17, 20.

EARC of Slane
Add: Earc as his father and, according to an early text, he was Ireland's fourth *athlaoch*, 'former layman'.[12] [p. 286, l. 4]
Add: Duleek.[14] His relics, presumably enshrined, were taken on tour in 776, and his crozier [p. 286, l. 8]
Add to note: 12 Anecd. iii, 60.

EARNÁN of Inis Caoin
Add: Given that Drumhome adjoins Kilbarron, which took its name from Bairrfhionn, the Earnán associated with the former church may be identical with the patron of Inis Caoin. [p. 287, end of entry]

ÉIGNEACH
Add: The saint may also have been patron of the Wexford church of Killegney.[3] [p. 288, l. 4]
Add (to) notes: 1 AnH 12, 84. 3 TNW 1112–13.

Add before **Éimhín** of Donaghmore: **Éimhearán** of Fenagh and Drumreilly, Co. Leitrim. Travelling in Co. Leitrim in 1836, John O'Donovan wrote that holy wells in the parishes of Fenagh and Drumreilly were dedicated to Éimhearán (anglicized Everaun and Everan), whom he thought to be the 'Mabhrán' left by Patrick at Domhnach Maighe Sleacht, now possibly a site at Kilnavert in the parish of Templeport, barony of Tullyhaw, Co. Cavan, which adjoins Drumreilly.[1] There is no record of this saint's feastday, but seven bishops of Drumreilly were remembered on 15 January.[2]

Add to notes: 1 *DKil* 403; *OSL* CN/LM 206; *BP* 1019–25; *VT* 92; *FL* 604–5. 2 *MartT* 8; *MartG* 16; *MartD* 16.

Éimhín of Monasterevin

Add: Cruach, now the townland and parish of Croagh in the Limerick barony of Connello Lower.[2] [p. 291, l. 14 of entry]

Add: Monasterevin and its freedoms. According to one account, the manner of his death was tantamount to martyrdom.[5a] [p. 291, l. 27 of entry]

Add: *án*, 'noble', though the association with *Áine* in a seventeenth-century poem may refer to Knockainy in the Limerick barony of Smallcounty.[9] [p. 292, l. 7]

Add to notes: 2 *HDGP* vi, 120. 5a *MartO* 260; *RC* 45, 166. 9 *FSPP* 80.

Eirnín of Cluain Deochra

Add: of Dunleckny.[5] At Cluain Deochra, he is said to have been visited by Féichín of Fore, who went on to free a mill near the guesthouse from a troublesome rattle.[6] [p. 292, l. 15 of entry] [Renumber notes 6 and 7 to 7 and 8]

Add: Nearer to Clonmacnoise, he may also have given name to St Erneen's well in the East Galway parish of Leitrim.[9] Eirnín died, according to the annals, in 635.[10] [p. 292, end of entry]

Add (to) notes: 1 ibid. 2.9, 27–30. 6 *ASH* 138. 9 *OSL* GY ii, 9. 10 *AU s.a.*

Add ahead of **Eirnín** *of Cranfield:* **Eirnín** of Corkaree. *See* Earnán of Drumhome.

Add ahead of **Elly:** **Eliva.** *See* Ailbhe of Shancough.

Eithne daughter of Baoth
Add to note: 3 *AH* 8, 19.

Eoghan of Ardstraw
Read: – improbably dated to the eighth or early ninth century – [p. 295, l. 8 of entry]

Add to notes: 3 *CHSC* 157–8. 17 *AnH* 12, 83. 18 *AnH* 12, 107, 109.

Eoghanán
Add to note: 2 *SBDeer* 383.

Eolang

Add: Múscraighe group,[3] and a poem of forty quatrains on God's anger is attributed to him in some manuscripts.[4] [p. 298, ll 16–17]

Add: recourse.[6] There is another well in the parish of Mourneabbey. [p. 298, l. 24]

Add to note: 3 *IrT* i, 36.

Add after **Eunan:** Everaun. *See* Éimhearán.

FACHTNA of Roscarbery
Add: an awareness of the connection brought about after 1177 by the movement of the Uí Dhonnabháin (O'Donovans) from south Limerick into Carbery, or of the more ancient ties [p. 300, l. 16]
Add: There is a well dedicated to the saint in the townland of Rossbrin, parish of Skull. [p. 300, end of entry]
Add to note: **4** *FNCC* 124.

FAITHLEACH
Add: His coarb was among the ecclesiastics entitled to be present at the inauguration of O'Connor as king of Connacht.[7] [p. 302, end of entry]
Add note: **7** *JRSAI* 2, 340; *MSPAG* 188–9.

FAOILEANN of Killeely
Add: A saint Faoile(ann) also gave name to the Wexford parish of Killila.[10] [p. 303, end of entry]
Add (to) notes: **8** *CKV* 60. **10** *TNW* 1120–1.

FAOLÁN of Aachen
Add: He gave name to 'Killilan' in the townland of Cahertinny and ~~H~~his feast was observed at 'Tobar Adhlain' [p. 304, l. 4]
Add to note: **6** *JGAHS* 6, 145.

FAOLÁN of Strathfillan
Add to notes: **2** *NSW* 187. **3** *LegSS* 22–6, 360; *NSW* 195–201.

Add after **Faolchú** son of Faolchar: **Farnan.** *See* Mothoiréan of Tullow.

FÉICHÍN of Fore
Add: for deriding the saint and, unusually in saints' Lives, ends with hymns in his honour.[17] [p. 310, l. 24]
Add: the coincidence of name, but there is a well dedicated to the saint at Lackan in the parish of Ballynakill.[22] [p. 310, l. 40]
Add: Traces of the saint's cult in Leinster are also found in the Ossory parishes of Sheffin, which takes its name from him, and Danesfort, where there was a site called 'Cill Fhéichín'.[28] Among the saint's relics was a bell, and his 'cursing stone' was preserved at Leac Fhéichín in the townland of Dooghta, parish of Cong.[28][29] Finally, Féichín was among the saints invoked as guarantors of the Law of Adhamhnán, and his name is also invoked in a poem attributed to Moling.[29][30] [p. 311, ll 5–6] [Renumber notes 28 and 29 as 29 and 30]
Add (to) notes: **17** 84–6 §22; *CL* 47–9. **22** *OSL GY* 516. **28** *HADO* ii, 326–7; iii, 389. ~~**28**~~ **29** *AFM s.a.* 1144; *JGHAS* 64, 5; *EMH* 485 §227. ~~**29**~~ **30** *CA* §22; *Anecd.* ii, 28 §1.

Add before **Feidhealm**: **Féichín** of Kilcrumper: Among the saints attached to the Leinster family of Dál gCormaic, alias Maca Cormaic, was a man named Mofhiacha, alias Fiacha, whose feast fell on 27 December.[1] The name *Féichín* is a diminutive of *Fiach(a)*, and it is scarcely a concidence that a namesake named Féichín Maca Luighbhe was remembered on the following day. The saint's attachment to the Maca Cormaic may explain the presence in the Cork parish of Kilcrumper of a now obsolete ecclesiastical site named Cill Fhéichín; the founding of Kilcrumper is attributed to Abán, the best-known of the saints assigned to the Maca Cormaic.[2]

Add notes: 1 *MartT* 1; *MartG* 248; *MartD* 348. 2 *CrC²* §4; *HDGP* iii, 171; *VSHH* 264 §17; *VSHP* i, 17 §22.

FEIDHLIMIDH of Kilmore

Add: named after him, and another (Toberfelim) in the Longford parish of Granard probably also takes its name from him.[8] [p. 313, l. 12]

Add: The saint's name was anglicized as both Phelim and Felix.[10] [p. 313, end of entry]

Add (to) notes: 8 OSL LD/WH i, 25. 10 *Breifne* 4, 202.

FEILIG FIONN

Read: Uí Chon Cheanainn (O'Concannons), first the east Galway parish of Moylough, later adjoining the approximate equivalent of the parish of Kilkerrin, north-east of Tuam.[2] [p. 313, l. 8 of entry]

Add to note: 3 *Ainm* 3, 3–4.

FEIME

Add: name as *Fernae/Fenicus* in an early [p. 314, l. 15 of entry]

Add to notes: 5 *Ainm* 3, 4. 6 *AnH* 12, 107, 109.

FEIRGHIL

Add to note: 2 *SAM* 11, 301–17; *OLL* 1, 21–2.

Add ahead of **Festy**: **Felix**. *See* Feidhlimidh of Kilmore.

FIAC

Read: ~~Echtarnach~~ Echternach in Luxembourg [p. 315, l. 32]

FIACHNA / FIACHRA

Add to note: 7 *JIA* 21, 139.

FÍNGHIN

Add: The 'Fingenus' remembered on 12 November in the martyrology of the Regensburg *Schottenkloster* may be the patron of Quin.[6] [p. 318, end of entry]

Add (to) notes: 4 *SAM* 24.1, 17, 19. 6 *FSHIM* 242; *MartR* 162.

FINCHEALL

Add to note: 4 *LegSS* 247, 362–3.

Add before **Finnéan**: **Finneach** of Dorn. *See* Sineach of Killinny.

FINNIAN of Clonard

Add: The saint's relics, presumably enshrined, were taken on tour in 776.[28] His coarb at the Roscommon church of Clooncraff was among the ecclesiastics entitled to be present at the inauguration of O'Connor as king of Connacht.[29] [p. 321, end of entry]

Add (to) notes: 22 cf. *BCML* 92 §90, 94 §92. 25 *FEMN* 363, 390. 28 *AU s.a.* 29 *JRSAI* 2, 340; *MSPAG* 189.

FINNIAN of Movilla
Add: A relic of his reached the Continent, where it was kept, arguably, at Ferrières in France or at a church in the Rhineland.[24] Another relic, accompanied by relics of Colum Cille and Adhamhnán, reached Saint-Maurice d'Agaune in the Swiss canton of Valais by the second half of the eighth century, and by the mid-ninth century another relic is attested for the Rhineland.[25] [p. 323, end of entry]

Add (to) notes: **16** LegSS 42–5, 422–3. **17** ASH 438; EA 189. **22** AnH 12, 85. **24** EIRD 55–68; RIW 15–19. **25** RIW 13, 32.

FIODHMHAINE
Add: Fiodhmhaine's death in 757 describes him as an anchorite; before this, in 744 and 748, what was presumably his Law (*lex nepotis Suanaigh*) had been twice proclaimed over the Northern Half of Ireland.[10] [p. 324, l. 35 of entry]
Add: Finnian of Clonard, whose church is elsewhere associated with 'Ua Suanaigh'.[15] A poem of prophecies also refers to one or other of the brothers, and 'Ó Suanigh' is among the mainly Connacht saints invoked in a poem by Donnchadh Mór Ó Dálaigh (†1244).[16] [p. 325, ll 11–12]

Add to notes: **15** BCML 78 §75. **16** DDé 51.

FÍONÁN of Teach Oirthir
Add to note: **3** cf. AB 76, 389, 401.

FÍONÁN CAM
Add: the Corca Dhuibhne of south Kerry to whom he bequeathed that they should never be without a famous nun.[25] [p. 329, l. 37]
Add: 14 September, and he was remembered at Nohavaldaly on the Cork-Kerry border on 14 December.[27] [p. 329, l. 39]
Add: Adhamhnán's reliquary, and his grave (*Leacht Fhíonáin*) was reputedly located on a hill in the Kerry parish of Killinane.[29] [p. 329, l. 41]

Add to notes: **25** ZCP 19, 175; PRIA 55C4, 83. **27** AB 53, 215. **29** UíR 51. **30** SAM 24.1, 17, 21.

FÍONÁN LOBHAR
Add: The saint was apparently also patron of the church in Malahide parish, adjoining Swords parish, and he was widely venerated in Scotland.[7] [p. 330, last line of entry]

Add to note: **7** AH 8, 22.

FIONNACHTA of Limerick
Add: Limerick city.[6] The Limerick parish of Killeenoghty and 'Chapelfeenaghty' [p. 331, l. 23]

FIONNBHARR of Cork
Add: September, including the Hebridean isle of Barra (27 September) and Dornoch in Caithness, where the Breviary of Aberdeen version of his Office Life appears to have been compiled.[18] [p. 334, l. 5]
Add: Cuimín of Connor and, as well as being lauded for his virtue in the face of carnal temptation, he was thought to be [p. 334, l. 12]

Add to notes: **18** BBa. 168–70; LegSS 234–7, 361–2. **20** Seanchas 235 §5

Add before **Fionnbharr** of Little Island: **Fionnbharr** of Kilruddery. *See* Fionnbharr of Killegar.

FIONNCHÚ
Add to notes: **1** *HMDC* 12–13. **13** cf. *BLCat.* i, 637.

FIONNLUGH of Doon
Add to note: **3** *AnH* 12, 83, 107, 109.

FIONTAN of Clonenagh
Add: Caoin) in the parish of Clonenagh, and possibly of the Dublin parish of Killo'grange (formerly Clonkeen), [p. 340, l. 39]
Add: He was patron of the Uí Mhórdha of Laois.[25] Furthermore, his relics were allegedly translated to Leighlin in 1348, with a view to having him canonised.[26] [p. 341, end of entry]
Add notes: **25** *FFÉ* iii, 112; **26** *AB* 104, 93.

FIONTAN FIONN
Add to notes: **6** *CSMA* i, 39. **9** *SAM* 2.1, 197.

FIONTAN MAOLDUBH
Add: An obit of 629 is assigned to Fiontan.[8] [p. 344, end of entry]
Add note: **8** *ATIg. s.a.* 628; cf. *CI* i, 137n.

FLANN of Derrynaflan
Read at note: **7** *ACoK* ~~37~~ 36.
Add to note: **6** *SAM* 24.1, 17.

FLANNAID
Add to note: **1** *HMDC* 13–14.

FLANNÁN
Add: The translation took place on 26 August, according to the martyrology of the Regensburg *Schottenkloster*.[30] [p. 349, end of entry]
Add (to) notes: **24** *SAM* 24.1, 17, 19. **30** *MartR* 123; *FSHIM* 240.

FOIRDEOIR
Read: The ~~otherwise unattested~~ abbot, who was otherwise remembered in the name of a well called 'Thobural Gyly' (*Tobar Ailghile*) to the east of the river Suck, may have been pressed into service
Add to note: **2** *COD* i, §258.

FORANNÁN.
Add: **Forannán.** *See also* Mothoiréan; Torannán.

FORANNÁN of Alternan
Add: The association of his church at Alternan with Boyle would suggest that he is the 'Arannán' invoked in a poem by Donnchadh Mór Ó Dálaigh (†1244), who died in the abbey of Boyle.[10] [p. 352, end of entry]
Add note: **10** *DDé* 50; *ACon.* 1244.7.

FORANNÁN of Donaghmore
Add: He may be the Forannán brought together with Déaglán in the 1528 litany of the Benedictines of Abingdon in England.[6] [p. 352, end of entry]
Add note: 6 *HBS* 119, 48.

FRAOCHÁN
Add: thirtieth year, and another version of this text assigns him to an unidentified place named Druim Dághanna in Dál nAraidhe in north-east Ulster.[2] [p. 354, l. 5 of entry]
Add to note: **2** *MartO'*169; *HDGP* viii, 19.

FUINCHE of Abbeylara
Add: She may also have given name to Clonfinfy (Cluain Fuinche) in the Longford parish of Killashee. [p. 355, end of entry]

FURSA
Add: Fursa, whose words of advice were included by Maol Ruain in his teaching of the daughter of a king 'in the eastern countries', and who guaranteed Molaga, the freedom of his *tearmann*, is alleged to have witnessed a company of angels leading to Heaven.[15] [p. 359, l. 16]
Add: Kilcoona, and he was also remembered in the neighbouring parish of Kilkilvery.[20] [p. 359, l. 31]
Read: Fursa died, according to the annals in 648/9, and his ~~The saint's~~ feast of 16 January is recorded in both continental and insular calendars and martyrologies.[23] A second feast, possibly that of the translation of his remains, fell on 9 February.[24] The vision attributed to him in his early Latin Life is dated by the Annals of Ulster to 627.[25] [p. 359, last two lines]
Add to notes: **2** *TBF*; *MGH.SRM* iv, 423–49; *VFBA* 1–21. **3** *FIO* 1–15. **17** *TEAB* 690 §5. **19** *SAM* 24.1, 17, 22. **20**, 276. **23** *AU s.a.* **24** *ASH* 282–300; *BiblSS* v, 1321; *DIB* iii, 1131–2. **25** *MGH.SRM* iv, 435; *AU s.a.*

GALL CRÁIBHTHEACH
Read: The saint died in 730, and b~~B~~y the early seventeenth century, Lullymore's patron was Patrick.[6] [p. 360, l. 16 of entry]
Add to note: **6** *AU s.a.*

GARAILT
Add: The form Gearóid was also used in a dedication in the townland of Temple, in the Galway parish of Clonkeenkerrill.[23] [p. 362, end of entry]
Add note: **23** *JGAHS* 60, 12.

GARBHÁN son of Aonghas
Add: saints' pedigrees, and in the late vernacular Life written for Forannán of Alternan.[2] [p. 363, l. 6 of entry]
Add to note: **2** *Anecd.* iii, 2 §3.

GEARMÁN
Add: **Gearmán**. *See* Diarmuid of Inchcleraun; Geamán.

Add before **Giolla Críost Ua Morgair**: **Giolla Aodha Ua Muighin**, bishop of Cork.
Bernard of Clairvaux, our only source of information for what transpired in 1140

after the death of Ua Sealbhaigh, successor of Fionnbharr, recounts in his Life of Maol Maodhóg (Malachy) how 'not one of the nobles of the country but rather a poor man ... and he happened to be an outsider' was elected bishop of Cork.[1] The 'poor man' left nameless by Bernard was Giolla Aodha, a Connachtman, hence his description as an 'outsider', who had formerly been a monk at Errew on Lough Conn in Co. Mayo.[2] As an intruder had never before come from so far away to assume the highest ecclesiastical office in Cork, it would seem that his accession was designed to serve principally as an instrument of church reform. Also, while still little more than a fledgling monastery, through Giolla Aodha's appointment the house of canons regular founded in 1137 had now thrust upon it the task of supervising Cork's ecclesiastical affairs for almost the whole of the remainder of the twelfth century.[3] Giolla Aodha was destined to give his name to the priory, later known as Gill Abbey (Mainistear Ghiolla Aodha) and, perhaps more importantly, his Connacht background arguably led to the adoption of a west of Ireland pedigree for his patron Fionnbharr.[4] Giolla Aodha also found himself obliged to oversee a radical reorganisation of the area under his jurisdiction. At the synod of Rathbrassil in 1111 Cork had been given control over a very large area extending roughly from the river Blackwater to the sea. At Kells-Mellifont in 1152, on the other hand, Cork was forced to cede considerable territory to the new dioceses of Cloyne and Ross. There is no evidence to show that Giolla Aodha resisted these sweeping changes; indeed, his presence at Kells-Mellifont among the signatories of the synodal decrees indicates that he acquiesced in them. Giolla Aodha died in 1172, but there is no record of the day of his death.[5] He is, however, included among mainly Connacht saints in a poem written by Donnchadh Mór Ó Dálaigh.[6]

Add notes: **1** BCLM 92. **2** AFM 1172. **3** MRHI 167–8. **4** MakS 66–7, 70–3. **5** AFM s.a. **6** DDé 51.

Gobán Fionn

Add: relics were reputedly kept, possibly in a church named 'ecclesia sancti Gauueni' after him.[3] [p. 368, l. 2]

Add: He died, according to the annals, in 661.[8] [p. 368, end of entry]

Add (to) notes: **3** MartD 424; CM 52. **8** ATig. s.a. 660.

Gobnaid

Add: Ballynahinch in the Limerick parish of Knocklong, and Castletown in the Limerick parish of Corcomohide [p. 368, l. 6 of entry]

Add: have survived, as has the bell associated with her.[9] [p. 369, l. 10]

Add to notes: **5** TH i, 63–5. **9** EMH 458 §156

Greallán Craoibheach

Add: Creeve, where his coarb later enjoyed the privilege of being present at the inauguration of the O'Connor kings of Connacht.[7] [p. 370, l. 22]

Add: Fiontan of Taghmon, and the Registry of Clonmacnoise assigns to him an unidentified church in Leinster named 'the monastery of Gryllan'.[11] [p. 370, l. 35]

Add to notes: **7** MSPAG 189. **11** RClon. 458. **12** TEAB 690 §4.

GRIOGHÓIR BÉALÓIR

Add: A poem in Irish on the Gregorian chant, which describes the Pope as 'Grioghóir, abbot of Rome from Ireland', provides him with the patronymic Tuileagnaidh.[6] Finally, Colmán Eala of Lynally is said to have received news of Gregory's death long before it otherwise reached Ireland, and a late poem asserts that Gregory granted Colum Cille abbatial authority over Ireland and Scotland.[7] [p. 317, end of entry]

Add (to) notes: **1** *RC* 46, 231; *RC* 49, 184–5. **6** *ZCP* 8, 115 §§23–4. **7** *VSHH* 215–16; *RC* 46, 249§15; *ZCP* 12, 373, 394 §24.

GUAIRE BEAG

Read: Gormus/Gromus.[5] [p. 371, last line of entry]

Add to note: **5** *AnH* 12, 81, 108, 110.

Add after **Hoult**: **Hugh**. *See* Aodh of Rahugh; Beoaidh of Ardcarn.

Add [at start of chapter]: **Ia** No saint of this name is known from the Irish lists of the saints but a person named Ia is thought to have given name to the Cornish church of St Ives, following the arrival of the saint's cult from the Breton church of Plouyé.[1] According to the extensive record that grew up about the cult in Cornwall, the saint was a disciple of Finbarr and this tradition, as well as the saint's name has given rise to the belief that she was patron of Killeagh, from *Ceall Ia* in the Cork barony of Imokilly.[2] Regrettably, however, no evidence has survived in the Irish record to show that *Ia* was ever used either as a personal name or as a lexical item.[3]

Add notes: **1** *SCorn.* 144–5. **2** *HMDC* 9–10; *Celtica* 29, 307. **3** *HDGP* iv, 3–4.

ÍDE

Read: In addition to ~~an early litany~~ three early litanies, including two of continental provenance, which ~~invokes~~ her name [p. 377, l. 23]

Add to note: **19** *SIHI* 189–90.

INGHEAN BHAOITH

Add: Her name may have been anglicized as Winifrid, alias Winnie, a very common name among females in the parish of Killinaboy. [p. 379, end of entry]

Add to note: **6** *SAM* 24.1, 17, 21.

IOBHAR of Begerin Island

Add: in the latter saint's Life, and a poem on Patrick's Purgatory addresses Iobhar together with Mochta and other saints.[11] [p. 381, last line]

Add to note: **11** *TEAB* 522.

IOTHARNAISC

Add to note: **2** *LegSS* 3–5, 11, 357–8; *SBDeer* 375–7.

LAICHTÍN

Read: Aghavallen ~~and~~, where, in John O'Donovan's time, people were in the habit of swearing by his arm (*dar láimh Laichtín*), at various holy wells in Clare, including those in Kilfarboy and Kilnamona, and at Donaskeagh in the Tipperary parish of Rathlynin.[9] [p. 387, ll 33–4 of entry]

Add: Joseph's substitution for Laichtín, as at Kilnamona in Co. Clare.[17] [p. 388, end of entry]

Add to notes: **9** *UL Camb.* Add. 622 (1, 2) 39; *ACE* 195. **11** *CKV* 60. **12** *SAM* 24.1, 17, 20.

LAIDHGEANN of Kyle

Read: Catholic Epistles, and it has been suggested that he was the successor of Molua (Lughaidh) of Kyle mentioned in Cummian's letter on the Easter question.[3] [p. 388, l. 9 of entry]

Add to note: **3** *IIAM* 589–91.

LAIGHNEACH

Add to note: **1** *Breifne* 4, 204.

LAISRÉAN of Durrow

Read: of ~~Mundrehid~~ Mondrehid (Mion) in the Laois parish of ~~Aghaboe~~ Offerlane.[5] [p. 389, l. 14 of entry]

LASAIR of Kilronan

Add: (O'Duignans), who may also have had charge of her miracle-working bell.[2] [p. 393, l. 8 of entry]

Add: the biographer of Náile, who was allegedly her teacher, to punish [p. 394, l. 11]

Add to notes: **2** *EMH* 481–2 §214. **11** *BLCat.* ii, 571.

LATIARAN

Add: Pilgrimage to Cullen is already attested in the early eighteenth century.[9] [p. 395, end of entry]

Add note: **9** *PnaB* 3811–13.

LIADHAIN daughter of Diarmuid

Add: and it has been suggested that she was patron of the Limerick parish of Killeely.[4] [p. 395, end of entry]

Add to note: **4** *NMAJ* 3, 108.

LÍTHGHIN

Read: parish ~~of Clonsast~~ and barony of ~~Coolestown~~ Geashill, Co. Offaly [p. 399, l. 1 of entry]

Add: him at Clonmore later became known as 'Balleenlawn church', while a nearby well gave name to the adjoining townland of Toberleheen.[3] [p. 399, ll 9–10] [Renumber notes 3 and 4 to 4 and 5]

Add note: **3** *AIOY* §§642, 759.

LOMÁN of Lough Gill

Add: his namesake at Calry on Lough Gill [p. 401, l. 10 of entry]

Add to notes: **8** *DEPPP* 338; *AH* 8, 38. **9** *AB* 46, 409–10.

LON GARADH
Add: Augustine of Hippo, a likening which has led to the suggestion that he may have been the Augustinus who wrote *De mirabilibus sacrae scripturae*.[2] [p. 402, l. 8 of entry]

Add to note: **2** *IIAM* 595.

LORCÁN
Add to note: **18** *PPPMI* 327–8.

LUAITHRINN
Add: The saint's feast fell on 8 June and she may also have been remembered on that day in Springlawn (*Cluain Luaithrinne*) in the Galway parish of Ballynakill, barony of Killian.[6] [p. 406, l. 12]

Add to note: **6** Logainm.ie 'Springlawn'.

LUCHTIGHEARN
Add: his mother Brígh, whose womb was allegedly blessed by Colum of Terryglass, [p. 407, l. 5]

Add: throughout Ireland, whereas the biographer of Colum of Terryglass described Luchtighearn as Colum's disciple.[5] [p. 407, l. 20]

Add: 25 July or, as the calendar in Maynooth manuscript M 84 asserts, 10 November.[10] [p. 407, l. 34]

Add to notes: **2** *VSSH* 230 §22. **4** *SAM* 24.1, 17, 20. **5** *VSSH* 230 §22, 231 §27. **10** Maynooth MS M 84, 229.

LUGHAIDH of Clonleigh
Read: corrupt (Latin) forms *Cluoghus, Douglus* and *Doughus* [p. 408, l. 12 of entry]

Add to note: **5** *AnH* 12, 109.

LUGHAIDH OILITHIR
Add: Muadhán may also have given name to Tymon in the Dublin parish of Tallaght.[5] [p. 410, l. 4]

Add note: **5** Logainm.ie 'Tymon'.

LUGHNA of Kiltrasna
Read: dedicated to him and, representing his church, he is among the saints said, tendentiously, to have owed tribute to Caillín of Fenagh.[4] [p. 410, l. 8 of entry]

Add to note: **4** *BFen*. 286.

LÚIREACH
Add: In an early seventeenth-century description of the diocese of Derry his name is written *Lourachus*.[12] [p. 411, last line]

Add (to) notes: **4** *SacH* 230–46. **12** *AnH* 12, 108, 110.

Add after **Lupait**: **Lúrán**. *See* Lúireach.

MAC CAILLE
Add: His obit is entered in the annals for 490 and his feastday was 25 April [p. 413, end of entry]

Add to notes: **1** *CI* i, 79n. **7** *AU s.a.*

Mac Caorthainn of Clogher

Add: rough ground, and a poem on Patrick's Purgatory addresses him and other saints.[4] [p. 413, l. 12 of entry]

Add: He died, according to the annals, in 506 and his relics, including a bell and a head-bone, were kept at Clogher.[14] [p. 414, end of entry]

Add (to) notes: **4** *TEAB* 522 §ff. **14** *AU s.a.*; *ClRec.* 7, 375; *EMH* 484–5 §224.

Insert before **Mac Cuilinn**: **Mac Creiche**. *See* Mac Reithe.

Mac Cuilinn

Add: September and holy wells were dedicated to him at Lusk and Grallagh in north Dublin.[7] Finally, his name is invoked in a poem attributed to Moling and, also, in a poem which locates him on Rathlin Island in Co. Antrim, together with three other saints, Colum Cille, Cainneach and Comhghall.[8] [p. 415, end of entry]

Add (to) notes: **7** *Rep.Nov.* 2, 75; *AHWD* 12. **8** *Anecd.* ii, 28 §1; *ZCP* 10, 53 §6.

Mac Cuill

Add: Finally, an anonymous poem in Welsh on St Mechyll of Llanfechell in Anglesey identifies its subject, opportunistically, as Mac Cuill of Man.[5] [p. 416, end of entry]

Add note: **5** *MWPSS* 70–2, 132–9.

Mac Dara

Add to note: **1** *OFWC* 97–9, 102.

Add after **Mac Earca**: **Mac Eirc** A saint of this name was associated with Teltown in Co. Meath, one of Ireland's three most famous places of assembly.[1] Together with Patrick and Ciarán of 'Carn', possibly the patron of Castlekieran, some ten miles west of Teltown, Mac Eirc reputably acted as a guarantor of the assembly.[2] According to the Annals of Ulster, relics of his were also brought to Teltown in 784.[3] Only one saint of the name is commemorated in the martyrologies, which assign him to 18 November and, in one case, place him in an unidentified church named Ceall Achaidh.[4]

Add note: **1** *Triads* 35; *SG* 73. **2** *MD* iv, 152. **3** *AU²* 784.9. **4** *MartG* 220; *MartD* 312.

Mac Liag

Add: A rector of the name Ua Donnghaile is, however, also recorded at Drumglass.[6] [p. 418, end of entry]

Add notes: **6** *AnnU* 15.

Mac Nise of Connor

Add: He died, according to the annals in 507, and h~~H~~is feastday [p. 419, last line of entry]

Add to note: **12** *AU s.a.*

Mac Reithe

Add to note: **9** *EMH* 466 §172.

Mac Táil

Add: It has been suggested that he was patron of the church of St Michells, on the river Poddle in the most ancient part of Dublin.[9] A relic of the saint reached the Continent, where it was kept, arguably, either at Ferrières in France or at some church in the Rhineland.[10] [p. 424, last line of entry]

Add notes: **9** *AH* 8, 14. **10** *EIRD* 55–68; *RIW* 15–19.

MAIGHNEANN

Add: Among other churches dedicated to Maighneann is Kilmactalway in the Dublin barony of Newcastle.[11] The saint's feast fell on 18 December.[††][12] [p. 425, last line of entry] [Renumber note 11 to 12]

Add note: **11** *AH* 8, 28; *PRIA* 97C 269.

MAINCHÍN of St Munchin's

Add: which, despite the reservations of some scholars, may mean [p. 426, l. 5 of entry]

Add to notes: **1** *NL* 169–70. **10** *SAM* 24.1, 17, 21.

MAINE of Aghanagh

Add: at Aghanagh, and a bell associated with the saint was preserved locally until the nineteenth century.[6] [p. 428, last line of entry]

Add to note: **6** *EMH* 482–3 §217.

Add before **Manach**: **Malachy**. *See* Maol Maodhóg.

MANCHÁN of Lemanaghan

Add to note: **10** *EIL* 28–30.

MAODHÓG of Clonmore

Add: St Mogue's in the townland of Glebe, near Clonmore, was held [p. 431, last line]

Add: not far from Clonmore, and at nearby Preban, where there is a well dedicated to him under the name of Aidan.[9] [p. 432, l. 3]

MAODHÓG of Ferns

Read: Inis Breachmhaighe, ~~the island of Port~~, an island on Brackley Lough in the Cavan parish of Templeport, a few miles north-east of Saint Mogue's Island on Templeport Lake and close to Drumlane [p. 432, ll 14–15 of entry]

Add: and Churchtown in the parish of Dysert (Díseart Nairbhre) [p. 434, l. 1]

Read: annals, in 620 ~~or~~, 625, or even 660, [p. 435, l. 25]

Add: In Leinster, Maodhóg also became patron of two Ossory parishes, Dunkitt and Dysartmoon.[52] [p. 435, last line of entry]

Add (to) notes: **45** *ATig. s.a.* 620, 659 / *AU s.a.* 625; *MartT* 13. **52** *HADO* iv, 137, 185.

MAOINEANN

Add: In Scotland, Maoineann possibly came to be known as Monan — of St Monan's in Fife — and as such became the subject of an Office Life, as found in the Breviary of Aberdeen, and of an entry in Hermann Greven's martyrology.[9] [p. 436, last line of entry]

Add (to) notes: **1** *TEAB* 445–51. **9** *LegSS* 62–4, 398–9; *AS. Iunii* vi, 121.

MAOL DALA

Add to note: **3** *SAM* 24.1, 17, 20.

MAOL DÓID
Add: named after the saint under the guise of 'Meldocius'.[9] [p. 435, end of entry]
Add to notes: **1** *ClRec*. 20, 473–90. **6** *ClRec*. 20, 488–9. **9** *ClRec*. 7, 406.

MAOL MAODHÓG
Add to note: **14** *SAM* 22.2, 8–24.

MAOL RUBHA
Add to note: **8** *LegSS* 196–9, 382–4; *SBDeer* 387–9.

MAOL TUILE of Dysart
Add: The 'Meltolinus' remembered on 8 November in the martyrology of the Regensburg *Schottenkloster* has not been identified.[7] [p. 447, end of entry]
Add (to) notes: **6** *EMH* 485 §226. **7** *FSHIM* 242; *MartR* 160.

MAOLÁN of Annagh
Add to note: **2** *Breifne* 4, 205–6.

MAOLÁN of Kilmoylan … Co. Galway.
Read: **Maolán** of ~~Kilmoylan (Ceall Mhaoláin), barony of Clare,~~ Killaspugmoylan in the Galway parish of Kilconickny. [p. 448, l. 1]
Add: Abbeygormacan, a little east of Killaspugmoylan.[2] [p. 448, l. 10]
Add: Kilmoylan in the Galway barony of Clare.[5] [p. 448, l. 17]

MAONACH of Dunleer
Add: rendered *Monachus*, and also into the martyrology of the Regensburg *Schottenkloster*, where the spelling is *Maenachi*.[8] [p. 449, end of entry]
Add to note: **8** *FSHIM* 241; *MartR* 150.

MAONAGÁN
Add: Maonagán's bell allegedly provided baptismal water for the child and the saint's feast [p. 449, l. 12 of entry]
Add to note: **4** *EMH* 482 §115.

MARCÁN
Add: local pilgrimage at the beginning of August.[2] [p. 449, end of entry]
Add note: **2** *LF* 3, 103–10.

Insert after **Masán**: **Mathona** of Shankill. *See* Beinéan of Kilbennan.

MEAL
Read: Meal's death is recorded for the year ~~488~~ 487, [p. 451, l. 6]

MEALLÁN
Add to note: **5** *OSL GY* i, 276.

MÉANÓG of Glenealy
Read: Tallaght, and a month later, on 30 January, he was remembered at Rosminogue.[3] [p. 452, l. 13 of entry]
Read note: **3** *MartT* 2, 13: *MartG* 26; 248; *MartD* 30, 350.

MEARNÓG of Aberchirder
Add to note: **1** *LegSS* 64–7.

MEARNÓG of Kilmarnock
Add to note: **1** cf. *LegSS* 250, 390–1.

Insert after **Mel**: **Meldocius**. *See* Maol Dóid.

MIODHAN
Add to note: **2** *ILL* 248.

MOBHEÓG of Artraighe
Add: on 16 December and, in view of the saint's maternal connection with the Déise, he could well be the patron named 'Mabiog', who is assigned to the church of Fews in the Waterford barony of Decies-without-Drum in a sixteenth-century unpublished, and unnumbered, copy of a Papal Bull preserved in the Archives of the Marques of Waterford at Curraghmore House, Co. Waterford.[3] [p. 457, last line of entry]
Add to note: **3** *AMW*.

MOBHÍ CLÁIRINEACH
Add: Gallen (from *Gaileanga*) and the Mayo parish of Kilmovee [p. 458, l. 12]
Add: from Colum Cille, with whom he also appears to have intervened on behalf of poets.[11] [p. 458, l. 26]
Add: A well dedicated to the saint was located in the townland of Grange in the Dublin parish of Holmpatrick.[14] [p. 458, end of entry]
Add (to) notes: **11** *DD* 221 §13. **14** *Rep. Nov.* 2, 73.

MOCHAMÓG
Read: **Mochamóg**. *See* Caimín of Inishcaltra; Mochomóg.

MOCHAOIMHE
Read: Flann son of Lonán, and he may also have been patron of Ballyogan in the south Dublin parish of Tully.[5] The saint ~~saint's~~ died, according to the annals, in 588, and his feast fell on 1 May.[6] [p. 459, l. 13 of entry]
Add to notes: **5** *Keimelia* 518. **6** *AFM s.a.* 584.

MOCHAOMHÓG of Leigh
Read: recalled the saint and the Kilkenny parish of Kilmakevoge was named after him.[19] [p. 460, l. 35]
Add to notes: **15** *AFM* i, 267n; *HADO* iv, 92. **19** *ASH* 589. **21** *LegSS* 80–3, 376. **23** (ii, 598).

Insert before **Mochaomhra**: **Mochaomhóg** of Inishglora. *See* Caomhán of Anatrim.

MOCHEALLÓG of Inch
Add: The name Giolla Mic Aoibhléin borne by a successor of Bréanainn of Clonfert and Ardfert, who died in 1166, reflects later Corca Dhuibhne devotion to the saint.[11] [p. 462, end of entry]
Add (to) notes: **10** *SAM* 24.1, 17, 21. **11** *AFM s.a.*

MOCHONNA of Feakle
Add: The saint appears to have also been venerated by the Clann Chon Mara (McNamaras) of Clare, albeit under the guise of Mochoinne.[4] [p. 464, end of entry]
Add (to) notes: **2** *SAM* 24.1, 17, 20. **4** *CoC* 40; *CT* i, 101.

Insert after **Mochonna** of Lusmagh: **Mochonna** of Monkstown, barony of Rathdown, Dublin. An Elizabethan fiant links the name Mochonna to the sub-townland of Carrickbrennan in the Dublin parish of Monkstown.[1] It is thought that this was the saint remembered on 13 January in the martyrologies, which assign him variously to Inchpatrick in the Dublin parish of Holmpatrick and a place called Leamhchoill, now possibly Longhill in the Wicklow parish of Kilmaconoge.[2]

Add notes: **1** *CPPI* 201. **2** *MartT* 7; *MartG* 14; *MartD* 14; cf. *Keimelia* 520.

MOCHONÓG of Kilmuckridge

Add: The saint may also have been patron of Timahoe in the Kildare parish of Clane, and ~~Tt~~the suggestion that his church may have been in Scotland has little to support it.[7] [p. 464, l. 20 of entry]

Add to note: **7** *CDKL* 241.

MOCHTA of Louth

Add to note: **9** cf. *CHSC* 157.

MOCHUA of Balla

Add: at death, which occurred, according to the annals, either in 638 or 694.[8] [p. 468, l. 4]

Add: A second feast, on 1 January, is noted in a calendar compiled by John Carpenter, archbishop of Dublin, and in an edition the same cleric prepared of Butler's *Lives of the Saints*.[14] [p. 468, end of entry]

Add (to) notes: **8** *AU s.a.*; *ATig. s.a.* 637. **9** *LisL* 4751–86; *LGen.* 276.10. **14** *RIA MS* 23 A 8, ii; *LIS* i, 24.

MOCHUA of Ticknevin

Add: named after the saint, and a church dedicated to him is recorded at Barreen in the Kildare parish of Balraheen.[4] [Renumber notes 4 and 5 to 5 and 6] [p. 469, l. 2]

Add note: **4** *CDKL* 261; Logainm.ie 'Barreen'.

MOCHUA of Timahoe

Add: Kildare.[11] Said by the annals to have died in 658, ~~Tt~~the saint [p. 470, l. 8]

Add to note: **12** *ATig. s.a.* 657.

MOCHUA LUACHRA

Add: The saint died, according to the annals, in 654.[6] [p. 470, end of entry]

Add note: **6** *AU s.a.*

MOCHUDA

Add: the saint's expulsion from Rahan in 636, [p. 472, l. 9]

Add: Roscrea – as echoed, perhaps, by Kilmacuddy in the parishes of Bourney and Killea, near Roscrea – and Athassel.[15] [p. 472, l. 15]

Add: At Burrow in the Dublin parish of Portraine, where a holy well was dedicated to him, he was also known as Cuddy.[31] The saint gave name to Kilmacot in the Wexford parish of Ballyvaldon.[32] [p. 473, end of entry]

Add (to) notes: **14** *AU s.a.* **31** *Rep. Nov.* 2, 80; *AHWD* 12, 20. **32** *TNW* 1137.

MOCHUIDBHRIOCHT
Add to note: **2** cf. *ASH* 679.

MOCHUILLE of Tulla
Add: 11 January, and his name was invoked in a Regensburg litany.[21] [p. 476, l. 12]
Add to notes: **17** *SAM* 24.1, 17, 19. **21** *CKV* 60.

MODHÍOMÓG of Glenkeen
Add: The saint's 'holy stone' stood on a hilltop at Graigue in the Tipperary parish of Dorrha, where he was known by the pet form of Díoma.[5] [Renumber note 5 to 6] [p. 477, l. 17]
Add: Without the support of any other source, the Four Masters assigned Modhíomóg and his brothers to 15 January.[7] [p. 477, end of entry]
Add (to) notes: **3** *DEPPP* 338. **5** *AITY* §1926. **7** *GRSH* 117 §9a.

Insert after **Modhíomóg** of Glenkeen: **Modhiúid** of Killamude. Neither the townlands of Killamude, which took their name from the saint, nor the parish in which they are located, namely Ballymacward in the barony of Tiaquin, have received much attention in the documentary record, a few lines only being devoted to the parish in the Ordnance Survey letters from Galway.[1] However, as *diúid* of the saint's name means 'simple', a West of Ireland glossator of the Martyrology of Aonghas took the opportunity of identifying the saint with a bishop named Simplex, remembered on 12 February in the Martyrology of Jerome.[2] The equation of the two was, however, correctly denied in another copy of the martyrology.[3]
Add notes: **1** OSL 'Galway', 62. *DIL* 'díuit'; *HDGP* iv, 24. **2** *MartO* 72. **3** *MartO* 72.

Add before **Modhomhnóg**: **Modhoma** of Kilmodum. *See* Díomán of Clonkeen.

MODHOMHNÓG OILITHIR
Add: Catalogue of the principal Irish saints [p. 478, l. 18]

MOGHEANÓG
Add: Mogheanóg, who may be the same as Mogheanóg of Ceall Chumhaile, a disciple of Finnian of Clonard.[3] [p. 479, l. 1]
Add to note: **3** *VSHH* 83 §5, 101 §19.

MOGHOBÓG
Add: Moghobóg of Ráith Lámhraighe, who is given first place in the Martyrology of Tallaght's list for 11 February, is also remembered on that day in the martyrology of the Regensburg *Schottenkloster*.[2] [p. 479, end of entry]
Add note: **2** *FSHIM* 234. *MartR* 29.

MOLAGA of Aghacross
Add to notes: **3** *HMDC* 14–17. **9** *EMH* 463–4 §162. **18** *CKV* 60, 64.83.

MOLAGA of Singland
Add to note: **5** *CKV* 60, 64.83.

MOLAISE of Devenish
Add: Relics of his, including shrine and crozier, are mentioned in an early prose-tale.[22] [p. 485, end of entry]
Add (to) notes: **5** *GILSL* 97–106. **16** *Peritia* 24–5, 230–40. **18** *FC* 233–5. **22** *Ériu* 35, 76 §12.

MOLING LUACHRA
Add: St Mullin's (Teach Moling), mainly in the barony of St Mullin's Lower, Co. Carlow, partly in the barony of Bantry, Co. Wexford. [p. 487, l. 1]
Add: Lugh, a christianized version of whom, Lúgadán by name, was patron of the Wexford parish of Templeludigan, adjoining St Mullin's and containing a townland named Monamolin (Muine Moling).[5] [p. 488, l. 15]
Add: A holy well at Corbally in the Dublin parish of Tallaght is also dedicated to Moling, as was the church that gave name to Kilmalin, formerly Stamelyn, in the neighbouring Wicklow parish of Powerscourt.[30] [p. 490, end of entry]
Add (to) notes: **5** *TNW* 1294, 1624–5. **22** *TEAB* 710. **30** *Rep. Nov.* 2, 85; *AHWD* 12; *Mdub.* xiii, 87.

MOLUA of Kyle
Add: Comhghall of Bangor, and a note added to the Martyrology of Aonghas gives a fanciful explanation of how he acquired his name.[23] [p. 492, l. 28]
Add to notes **8** *Peritia* 24–5, 90–107. **23** *MartO²* 180–2. **27** *EMH* 329–30 §21.

MOLUA son of Maonach
Read: Ross), and he probably gave name to 'Island-Molloe', now Horse Island in the parish of Castlehaven.[2] [p. 493, l. 6 of entry]
Add to note: **2** Logainm.ie 'Horse Island'.

MOLUÓG
Add to note: **4** *LegSS* 148–58, 395–8; *SBDeer* 387–9.

Add ahead of **Moneasóg**: **Monan**. *See* Maoineann.

MONINNE
Add: The saint's age at death is reputed to have been 180.[27] [p. 497, end of entry]
Add (to) notes: **9** *CI* i, 88n. **21** *TNW* 1141–2. **22** *EMH* 487 §232. **27** *MartD* 185; *Ériu* 13, 66 §63.

MORÓNÓG of Inishloe
Add: recorded of Morónóg, other than his presence at the court of Guaire son of Colmán at Dungory in the Clare parish of Kinvarradoorus together with Cuimín Fada of Clonfert, but among the holy wells [p. 498, l. 7]
Add (to) note: **2** *Ériu* 5, 28.

MOTHAGRA
Add to note: **4** *TNW* 1677–8.

MOSHEANÓG of Ballaghmoon
Read: the saint but, in view of his east Leinster connections, he may also have been patron of Kilmannock in the Wexford parish of Kilmokea.[4] [p. 499, l. 9]
Add to note: **4** *TNW* 1143.

MOSHIOLÓG
Read: He was again remembered on 25 July, where he is described as Moling's pupil.[3] [p. 500, end of entry]

Add note: 3 *MartT* 58; *MartG* 142; *MartD* 202.

MOSHIONA
Read: The hypocoristic form ~~Mioshiona~~ Moshiona [p. 500, l. 1 of entry]

MOSHIONA of Ballyman
Add to note: 1 *Keimelia* 520.

MOTHOIRÉAN of Tullow
Add: of Forannán (Farannán, anglicized Farnan), [p. 501, l. 17]
Add: A short office Life of the saint is preserved in the Breviary of Aberdeen.[8] [p. 501, end of entry]

Add note: 8 *LegSS* 141–3, 418–20.

MOTHRIANÓG
Read: Rúscach, near Carlingford in the Cooley [p. 501, l. 8 of entry]

MUGHAIN of Lyons
Add to note: 9 *SAM* 24.1, 17, 21.

MUIRCHÚ
Read: Both ~~O~~of Patrick's ~~two~~ seventh-century biographers, Muirchú (also written Murchú) and Tíreachán, ~~only the former~~ came to be regarded as saints. ~~He~~ Muirchú is included [p. 503, ll. 1–4]
Add: text of its kind, whereas the name Tíreachán is entered at 3 July in the Martyrology of Gorman, presumably in reference to the biographer, and added from there to the Martyrology of Donegal.[1] [p. 503, l. 5 of entry]
Add: Uí Fhaoláin of Kildare, Muirchú's affiliation to [p. 503, ll. 7 of entry]
Add: Armagh, unlike Tíreachán who appears to have been a native of Tirawley in north Connacht.[2] [p. 503, l. 9]
Add: No year of death is recorded for Tíreachán, who claims to have been a fosterling and pupil of Ultán, presumably of Ardbraccan.[5] [p. 503, end of entry]

Add (to) notes: 1 *MartT* 8; *MartO²* 139; *MartG* 112, 128; *MartD* 148, 184; *DIB* vi, 736–7; ix, 378–9; *BiblSS* ix, 666–8; xii, 499. 2 *MartO²* 144; *MartO¹* 99; *ASH* 465.31–2; *Kenney* 332; *CeltT* 87–9. 3 *CA* 18 §28; *Peritia* 1, 196. 4 *MartU* 243. 5 *PTBA* 124.

MUIRDHEABHAIR of Dysert
Add to notes: 2 *StH* 20, 119n. 6 *LegSS* 262–3, 356.

MUIREADHACH of Banagher
Add to note: 3 *AnH* 12, 83, 108, 110

MUNNA of Taghmon
Add to notes: 13 *TEAB* 640 §251. 25 *LegSS* 248–50, 400–1.

NÁILE
Add to notes: 8 *MGF* 23 §1. 9 *EMH* 473–4 §187.

NATHÍ of Taney
Add: in Taney, and the saint's church was in the townland of Dundrum.[4] [p. 512, end of entry]
Add to note: **4** AbEMLS 171–86.

NEACHTAN of Dungiven
Add to notes: **4** LegSS 20–3, 401–2. **5** cf. SBDeer 368–72.

NEAMH of Drumtullagh
Add: Neamh died, according to the Annals of Tighearnach, in 540.[3] [p. 513, end of entry]
Add note: **3** ATig. s.a.

NEAMHNAD
Add: of ~~Clonmore~~ (Cluain Mór Lughnadh), now possibly Clonmore in the parish of Kildalkey [p. 513, l. 1 of entry]

NEASÁN of Mungret
Add: a moral issue, and the biographer of Colum of Terryglass gave his subject the privilege of acting as intermediary between Neasán and God.[3] [p. 514, last line]
Add: According to some annals, Neasán died in 556/7.[15] [p. 515, last line of entry]
Add (to) notes: **3** VSHH 129–30 §50; ibid. 230–1 §24; VSHP i, 61–2 §42. **11** SAM 24.1, 17, 21. **12** CKV 60. **15** AI, ATig. s.a.; AFM s.a. 551.

NINNIDH LÁIMHDHEARG
Add to note: **2** EMH 400–1 §93.

ODHRÁN, charioteer
Add: A well in the townland of Clonmore in the Meath parish of Castlejordan, which mears with the counties of Offaly and Kildare, was named after the saint.[3] [p. 518, end of entry]
Add note: **3** OSL MH 216.

ODHRÁN MAIGHISTIR
Add to note: **4** VSHH 232 §28.

OILEARÁN SAPIENS
Add: his first name (sometimes written Oirearán) [p. 520, l. 1]
Add to notes: **1** BiblSS i, 644–5. **7** TEAB 690 §2.

OILILL of Movilla
Add: Bishop Oilill who died in 526 (or 536) and was [p. 521, l. 4]
Add to note: **3** AU s.a.

OIREANNÁN
Add to note: **1** BiblSS i, 643–4

OSÁN
Add: A holy well named 'St Assan's' at Raheny in the Dublin parish of the same name may also be dedicated to him.[4] [p. 522, end of entry]
Add note: **4** Rep. Nov. 2, 78; AHWD 12, 73; LIS iv, 512–13.

OSNAD
Read at note: **8** ZCP 5, 21–3.

PALLADIUS
Read at note: **2** CI i, 63.

Add to notes: **12** SBDeer 387. **13** LegSS 168–71, 406–7. **19** IP 157–90.

PATRICK
Read: Taberniae / Taburniae', a place ~~somewhere in Britain but yet to beidentified satisfactorily~~ sometimes thought to have been in Britain, but more likely to have been in the area about Boulogne-sur-Mer in north-western France.[1] [p. 527, ll 5–6 of entry]

Read: silva Focluti, ~~arguably~~ located either in the Mayo barony of Tirawley or, more likely, in the area about Slemish in Co. Antrim, [p. 527, ll 10–11]

Add: four laws of Ireland, and he is said to have assisted in drawing up the collection of early Irish law known as *Seanchas Mór*.[45] [p. 530, l. 40]

Add to notes: **1** IP 54–74. **7** TEP. **8** IP 130–2. **13** MedAE 43.3, 2219–33. **21** IKHK 232; ITS SS 23, 117–53. **38** Rep. Nov. 2.1, 6–16; cf. MDub. 18, 148–9. **45** Ériu 45, 5–13. **46** SaintP 29–33.

PUPA
Add: The saint died, according to the annals, in 655.[9] [p. 532, end of entry]

Add note: **9** AU s.a.

RIAGHAIL of Illaunmore
Add: The Tyrella saint was possibly also the author of a poem on the death in 704 of Aldfrith of Northumbria, which is attributed to Riaghail of Bangor.[8] [p. 535, end of entry]

Add (to) notes: **3** TEAB 690 §6. **8** FAI §165.

RÍCEALL
Add to notes: **4** OC 37, 37. **6** SAM 24.1, 17, 22.

ROC
Add: attested, and the 'cursing stone' at Salrock is named after the seven daughters of the king of Britain.[2] [p. 537, end of entry]

Add note: **2** JGAHS 65, 6.

RÓNÁN of Dromiskin
Add: A note added to the entry for 19 November in a twelfth-century version of the Martyrology of Usuard, kept in Canterbury, states that Rónán's arm was kept as a relic there.[22] [p. 540, end of entry]

Add (to) notes: **12** MKM 313; BCC 382 §355; RC 26, 134 §4. **13** Ériu 5, 78; LSLC 299. **22** VSHP ii, 240n; Propug.CV 981.

ROS
Add to note: **3** TEAB 690 §5.

RUADHÁN of Lorrha
Read: the second of which ~~curiously~~ presents him as ~~abbot of~~ being in Clonard.[17] [p. 543, ll 23–4]

Add: Regensburg in the ~~late~~ mid-twelfth century, [p. 543, l. 41]

Add: Ruadhán was patron of the Uí Chinnéidigh (O'Kennedys) and among his relics was a bell, now in the British Museum.[26] A note attached to the *Kilkenniensis* version of Ruadhán's Life states that his arm was kept as a relic in Canterbury, but this is more likely to have been the arm of Rónán of Dromiskin.[27] The shrine of the Stowe Missal, now in the National Museum but formerly kept at Lorrha, may also have come to be regarded as a relic of the saint.[28] [p. 543, end of entry]

Add (to) notes: **22** SAM 24.1, 17, 20. **26** FFÉ iii, 112. **27** VSHP ii, 240n; *Propug.CV* 981. **28** PRIA 91C10, 285–95.

SAMHTHANN

Add: barren mother, mention of all of whom has led to the implausible suggestion that the Life itself was compiled in the late eighth century.[6] [p. 546, l. 4]

Add: and a druid-poet, and she, representing her church, is among the saints said, tendentiously, to have owed tribute to Caillín of Fenagh.[11] [p. 546, l. 22]

Add to notes: **4** StC 20–1, 79. **6** MHA 101. **7** VSHP ii. 255 §10, 260–1 §26, 259 §19, 258 §18, 259–60 §23. **11** BFen. 286. **12** DDé 50.

SANTÁN

Read: Coleraine, and a note added to the entry on the saint's feastday in May attaches him to Drumline in the Clare barony of Bunratty Lower.[7] [p. 547, l. 10]

Add to note: **7** MartO¹ 85.

SÁRÁN of Tisaran

Read: Clonmacnoise, but he is mentioned in the *Registry of Clonmacnoise*, which devotes several lines to the 'holy cleark' named Sárán who built the church called *Teach Sáráin*, now Tisaran. [p. 548, l. 6]

Add to notes: **4** JRSAI 4, 449; CCLC 311. **6** OSL OY 159.

SÁRNAD daughter of Aodh

Add to note: **9** SAM 24.1, 17, 21.

SCOITHÍN

Add: Scoithín, including the proximity of his church to Clara, whose patron was identical with Colmán of Kilroot, the first church to be founded by Ailbhe in Ireland.[2] [p. 551, l. 8 of entry]

Add to notes: **2** VSHH 123 §22; HADO iii, 353. **9** RC 36, 287; 37, 351 §7.

Sáadna, bishop. *See* Libhréan ~~son of Dall~~ of Inis Mór.

SEANACH of Aghagower

Add: The Seanach invoked in a poem by Donnchadh Mór Ó Dálaigh may also refer to him.[5] [p. 554, end of entry]

Add (to) notes: **1** PTBA 150 §37.2–3. **5** DDé 50.

SEANÁN of Laraghbryan

Read: 2 September.[3] Although possibly selected through confusion with a Nicomedian saint named Zeno, this was [p. 557, l. 12]

Add to note: **4** Ainm 3, 6–7.

SEANÁN of Scattery Island
Add: *Salmanticensis* and the fifteenth-century *Kilkennienis*, [p. 557, last line]
Add: preserved in five manuscripts, including the mid-fifteenth [p. 558, l. 8]
Add: Seanán's birth at a place called Magh Lagha, now Moylough in the parish of
Kilrush.[12] [p. 558, l. 29]
Add to notes: **7** *AB* 66, 199–204. **9** *SS* 116–18; *ASH* 602–11. **12** *LisL* 1887–9, 1895. **31** *CKV* 64.78.

SEANÁN LIATH
Add: A dedication to the saint is also attested in the west Limerick parish of
Croagh.[3] [p. 560, end of entry]
Add note: **3** *PRIA* 25 C 411 §200; 412 §206.

SEANCHÁN
Add to note: **6** *AFM* v, 1456n.

Insert before **Seanphádraig**: **Seanchuimín**. *See* Cuimín Fada of Clonfert.

SEARBH
Add to note: **4** *LegSS* 158–62, 414–16.

Insert before **Sheemoge**: **Sheelin**. *See* Síolán.

SINEACH of Killinny
Read: (Ceall ~~Shinche~~ Fhinnche, formerly [p. 564, l. 1]
Add: Alternatively, she has been confused with Finneach of Dorn, who gave name
to Killinny, and who was remembered on 2 February.[4] [p. 564, end of entry]
[Renumber note 4 to note 5]
Add note: **4** *HDGP* iii, 172; *MartT* 14; *MartO* 58.

SINEALL of Cleenish
Add: Náile's church, and a poem on Patrick's Purgatory addresses him and other
saints.[5] [p. 565, l. 13 of entry]
Read at note: **2** ~~IV~~ *VCol.* 69 §3; *SCO* xviii.
Add to note: **5** *EBMEI* 522 §ff.

SINEALL of Clonpriest
Add to note: **5** *TNW* 1161–2

SÍOLÁN of Áth na gCeall
Add: Síolán (anglicized Sheelin) may also be the saint remembered — allegedly
on 4 May — at Kiltillane in the Tipperary parish of Templemore.[4] [p. 566, end of
entry]
Add note: **4** *ACE* 280; *Ainm* 3, 7.

SOICHEALL
Add: Soicheall's coarb was among the ecclesiastics present at the inauguration of
O'Connor as king of Connacht.[7] [p. 567, end of entry]
Add note: **7** *JRSAI* 2, 340; *MSPAG* 189.

SUBHALACH
Add to note: **3** *SAM* 24.1, 17, 21–2.

TALMHACH

Add: As the latter feast was followed by that of some sons of Neasán, who gave name to the island of Ireland's Eye, alias Inis Mac Neasáin, the 'S. Talmani' inscribed on a silver tongue (*lingula*) attached, according to James Ussher, to the Garland of Howth manuscript may refer to the Talmhach remembered on 14 March.[5] [p. 570, end of entry]

Add note: **5** *WWRJU* vi, 531.

TAOIDE

Add to note: **1** *AnH* 12, 108, 111.

TIGHEARNACH of Clones

Add: A stone cross in his memory stood at Donaghmoyne, the church of Lasair and Ciar, and ~~H~~he was also remembered [p. 573, last full line of entry]

Add to notes: **1** *TC* 67–80. **7** *TC* 87–91. **11** *TC* 55–6. **19** *EMH* 480 §210. **22** *CLRec.* 7, 404.

Insert after **Tighris**: **Tíreachán**. *See* Muirchú.

TOCHOMHRACHT

Add: July.[4] The Leitrim church was among the possessions claimed by Clonmacnoise in Connacht, and the saint's cult travelled as far as Corcomroe in Clare, where a parish (Kiltoraght) is named after her.[5] [p. 575, ll 14–15 of entry]

Add (to) notes: **2** *EMH* 478 §200. **5** *CCLC* 242.

TOLA CRÁIBHTHEACH

Read: martyrologies.[5] Tola's relics, presumably enshrined, were taken on tour in 793, and his crozier [p. 576, l. 2]

Add to note: **6** *AU s.a.*

TRENA

Read: **Trena**. *See* Trian of ~~Donoughmore~~ Donaghmore.

Add after **Triallach**: **Trian** of Brosna. *See* Trian of Donaghmore

TRIAN of Donaghmore

Add: As Patrick was leaving Munster, immediately after he had dealt with the ruling family of Múscraighe Tíre, he was entertained, according to the Tripartite Life, by Trian, a pilgrim *de Romanis*, 'of the Romans', at 'Craobhacha' near 'Brosnacha'.[4] The association with Múscraighe suggests that Trian of Donaghmore is intended and the site in question may now be Brosna in the Offaly parish of Kilmurryely.[5] [p. 577, end of entry]

Add notes: **4** *BP* 2545–55; *VT* 216. **5** *HDGP* ii, 202–3.

TRIAN son of Deadh

Add: Trian's relics were brought on circuit in 743, when the *bolgach* disease was rampant, and again in 794.[3] [p. 577, end of entry]

Add note: **3** *AU s.a.*

TROSCÁN

Add: It has been suggested that Drostán of Deirtheach, who died at Ardbraccan in 719, was identical with Troscán.[4] [p. 577, end of entry]

Add (to) notes: **3** *TMD* 35–8. **4** *AU s.a.*; *SBDeer* 382–4; *LegSS* 353.

UIDHRE

Add: a certain Uuiro (Wiro), alias Bearaidh, [p. 580, l. 7 of entry]

Add: A diminutive form of the saint's name, Uidhrín, may be preserved in the townland name Derryiron in the Offaly parish of Ballyburly.[4] [p. 580, end of entry]

Add (to) notes: **3** *TMD* 1–17, 175–8. **4** *ILL* 265–6.

ULTÁN of Ardbraccan

Add: died in 657 (or 663).[12] [p. 581, l. 30]

Add: The saint's relics, presumably enshrined, were taken on tour in 785.[17] [p. 581, end of entry]

Add note: **17** *AU s.a.*

USAILLE

Add: Usaille died, according to the annals, in 459.[11] [p. 582, end of entry]

Add note: **11** *AU s.a.*

Insert after **Vauk**: **Virgilius**. *See* Feirghil.

Insert after **Vogue**: **Winifrid/Winnie**. *See* Inghean Bhaoith.

INDEX OF PARISHES

Fenagh, b. Leitrim, LM. *Add*
Éimhearán

Fews, b. Decies-without-Drum, WD.
See Mobheóg of Artraighe

Geashill, b. Geashill, OY. *Add*
Líthghin

Glenkeen, b. Kilnamanagh Upr, TY.
Add Baodán of Killoscobe; Sárán
son of Brónach

Grallagh, b. Balrothery W., DB. *See*
Mac Cuilinn

Granard, b. Granard, LD. *Add*
Feidhlimidh of Kilmore

Holmpatrick, b. Balrothery E., DB.
Add Baodán of Cloney;
Mochonna of Monkstown

Inishcaltra, GY. *Add* Caolán of
Inishcaltra

Inishmagrath, LM. *See* Beoaidh of
Ardcarn

Kilbarron, b. Tirhugh, DL. *Add/Read*
Beag Bile; Cairbre of
Coleraine/Kilcarbry

Kilbarrymeaden, b. Decies without
Drum, WD. *See* Bairrfhionn of
Midíne

Kilclooney, b. Fews Lower, AH. *See*
Colmán of

Kilconickny, bb
Athenry/Dunkellin/Loughrea,
GY. *Add* Maolán of
Killaspugmoylan

Kilcrumper, b. Fermoy, CK. *Add*
Féichín of

Kilcummin, b, Moycullen, GY. *Add*
Breacán of Inishmore

Kilfenora, b. Corcomroe, CE. *Add*
Caimín of Inishcaltra

Kilkilvery, b. Clare, GY. *See* Fursa

Killaghtee, b. Banagh, DL. *See* Conall
of Inishkeel

Killashee, b. Moydow, LD. *Add*
Fuinche of Abbeylara

Killea, b. Ikerrin, TY. *See* Mochuda

Killeedy, b. Glenquin, LK. *Add*
Luchtighearn

Killeenoght, b. Pubblebrien, LK. *See*
Fíonnachta of Limerick

Killegney, b. Bantry, WX. *See* Éigneach

Killester, b. Coolock, DB. *See* Brighid
of Kildare

Killila, b. Ballaghkeen, WX. *See*
Faoileann of Killeely

Killilagh, b. Corcomroe, CE. *See*
Breacán of Aran

Killo'grange, b. Rathdown, DB. *See*
Fiontan of Clonenagh

Killury, b. Clanmaurice, KY. *See*
Lúireach

Kilmactalway, b. Newcastle, DB. *See*
Maighneann

Kilmahon, b. Imokilly, CK. *See*
Aighleann

Kilmakevoge, b. Ida, KK. *See*
Mochaomhóg of Leigh

Kilmodum, b. Fassadinin, KK. *See*
Díomán of Clonkeen

Kilmokea, b. Shelbourne, WX. *See*
Mosheanóg of Ballaghmoon

Kilmurryely, b. Clonlisk, OY. *See* Trian
of Donaghmore

Kilnahue, b. Gorey, WX. *Add* Curcach
of Kilcorkey Graveyard

Kinvarradoorus, b. Kiltartan, GY. *Add*
Morónóg of Inishloe

Knockainy, b. Smallcounty, LK. *Add*
Éimhín of Monasterevin

Leitrim, b. Leitrim, GY. *See* Eirnín of
Cluain Deochra

Loughmoe E., b. Eliogarty, TY. *See* Coga

Magheraculmoney, b. Lurg, FH. *Add*
Cuana of Eóinis

Malahide, b. Coolock, DB. *See* Fíonán
Lobhar

INDEX OF OTHER PLACES

Abingdon, England. *Add* Forannán of
Donaghmore
Aghkeran, RN. *See* Ciarán of
Clonmacnoise
Ailsa Craig, Scotland. *See* Donnán
Altamuskin, TE. *See* Cormac son of
Eachaidh
Asia Minor. *See* Feime. Cf. Chalcedon
Assaroe, DL. *Add* Conán son of
Tighearnach
Austria. *See* Feirghil of Aghaboe;
Fionnlugh. Cf. Salzburg;
Schottenklöster; Great Austrian
Legendary (under Subjects)

Ballinagleragh, LM. *See* Beoaidh of
Ardcarn
Ballykinvarga, CE. *See* Caimín of
Inishcaltra
Ballyogan, DB. *See* Mochaoimhe
Balrathboyne Glebe, MH. *See* Baoithín
of Iona
Barra, isle of, SCO. *See* Fionnbharr of
Cork
Barreen, KE. *See* Mochua of
Ticknevin
Baunaghra, LS. *See* Aodhán of
Eachradh
Beckery, Somerset, England. *See*
Brighid of Kildare
Belgium. *See* Odhbha. Cf. Brabant;
Fosses; Gheel; Liège; Nivelles;
Odenrode; Rolduc; Saint-Feuillen
du Roeulx; Stavelot
Boulogne-sur-Mer, France. *See* Patrick
Brabant, Belgium. *See* Odhbha
Brosna, OY. *See* Trian of Donaghmore

Bruckless, DL. *See* Conall of Inishkeel
Brycheiniog, Wales. *See* Cairbre
Oilithir; Cairinne; Caomhán
Oilithir; Díona; Díoraidh;
Dubhán; Eallóg; Iast; Mochonóg;
Moghoróg; Pán
Buryan, Cornwall. *See* Briúinseach

Cahertinny, GY. *See* Faolán of Aachen
Canon Island, CE. *Add* Colum of
Terryglass; Rónán of Dromiskin;
Ruadhán of Lorrha
Carrickbrennan, DB. *See* Mochonna
of Monkstown
Churchtown, WD. *See* Maodhóg of
Ferns
Cloonfinfy, LD. *See* Fuinche of
Abbeylara
Corbally, DB. *See* Moling
Cork, CK. *Add* Giolla Aodha
Cornwall. *See* Acobhrán; Cairneach of
Dulane. Cf. Buryan; Padstow; S.
Keverne
Croaghpatrick, MO. *Add* Brighid of
Kildare

Davy's Island, FH. *See* Cuana of Eóinis
Derryiron, OY. *See* Uidhre
Dooghta, GY. *See* Féichín
Doonane, LS. *See* Abán
Dornoch, SCO. *See* Fionnbharr of Cork
Drumlish, LM. *Recte* RN
Dunblane, Scotland. *Add* Bairrfhionn
of Aughkiletaun
Dundrum, DB. *See* Nathí of Taney
Dungory, CE. *See* Morónóg of Inishloe
Dunkellin, GY. *See* Caimín of Inishcaltra

INDEX OF ALTERNATE

(Mainly Anglicized) Names

INDEX OF SUBJECTS

Arm. *See* Relics

Athlaoich. Add Caimín of Inishcaltra

Bell. *See* Relics

Burial practice. *Elevation and translation of remains: Add* Fiontan of Clonenagh

Canonisation. *See* Fiontan of Clonenagh

Cistercian(s). *Add* Athracht

Cross / crucifix. *Add* Tighearnach of Clones

Great Austrian Legendary *See* Ailbhe of Emly; Flannán; Íde; Mochuille of Tulla; Rónán of Dromiskin; Seanán of Scattery

Inauguration. *See* King(s)

King(s).

    Inauguration. Add Bearach; Beoaidh of Ardcarn; Bréanainn of Clonfert; Brighid of Kildare; Caillín of Fenagh; Colmán of Mayo; Faithleach; Finnian of Clonard; Soicheall

Law (*cáin*). *Add* Bréanainn of Clonfert

Nun(s). *Add* Fíonán Cam

Poet/ry. *Add* Mobhí Cláirineach

Relics.

    Bréanainn of Clonfert; Brighid of Kildare; Cainneach of Aghaboe; Caoimhghin; Ciarán of Clonmacnoise; Comhghall of Bangor; Cuimín Fada of Kilcummin; Donnán; Finnian of Clonard; Fiontan of Clonenagh; Mac Táil

    Arm. Add Ciarán of Seirkieran; Rónán of Dromiskin; Ruadhán of Lorrha

    Bell. Add Adhamhnán; Beoaidh of Ardcarn; Brighid of Kildare; Ciarán of Seirkieran; Domhanghart; Gobnaid; Lasair of Kilronan; Mac Caorthainn of Clogher; Maine of Aghanagh; Maonagán; Ruadhán of Lorrha

    Glúnán. See Domhanghart. Cf. *Knee* below

    of Peter and Paul. See Colum of Terryglass; Cuimín Fada of Kilcummin; Palladius; Tighearnach of Clones

Schottenklöster. Add Dodhrán

Swear by/upon. *See* Bearach; Damhnad; Ciarán of Seirkieran; Éimhín; Laichtín; Mochta of Louth; Mura

Union (*Aonta/Fraternitas/*covenant). *Add* Cairneach; Cormac of Durrow

Vision(s)/dream/*baile. Add* Fursa

INDEX OF FEASTDAYS